VEGAS
LIVE AND IN PERSON

VE
LIVE AND

TEXT AND PRINCIPAL PHOTOGRAPHY BY

ABBEVILLE PRESS

GAS
IN PERSON

Jefferson Graham

PUBLISHERS NEW YORK

DEDICATED TO

THE MEMORY OF DAVE GRANOWSKY

AND THE

"GRANOWSKY DISPOSITION"

Editor: **Alan Axelrod**

Designer: **Nai Y. Chang**

Production supervisor: **Hope Koturo**

Published in the United States of America in 1989 by
Abbeville Press, Inc. First edition

**Library of Congress Cataloging-in-
Publication Data**

Graham, Jefferson.
    Vegas, live and in person / Jefferson Graham.
       p. cm.
    Bibliography: p.
    Includes index.
    ISBN 0-89659-945-0
    1. Las Vegas (Nev.)—History. 2. Gambling—
       Nevada—Las Vegas.
    I. Title.
    F849.L35G73   1989
    979.3' 13—dc 19

PHOTO THIS PAGE:
Murillo and Uliyses in performance

PHOTO OPPOSITE:
Showgirl in Siegfried and Roy's *Beyond Belief*

CONTENTS

6

Foreword

Las Vegas, says Bill Cosby, isn't really an American city.

> It couldn't be, because Americans wouldn't do this to other Americans. Communists would. Communists would move in, put these hotels in, and allow Americans to come in, lose their money, and go home. Good Americans wouldn't do that.

In any case, Las Vegas is the only American city whose unofficial founding father is a New York gangster. Bugsy Siegel developed Vegas as the incarnation of a mobster's vision of utopia: legal gambling, abundant supplies of women, drink, and song—and no clocks, just twenty-four hours of fun and frolic in the sand.

The seventieth-largest city in the United States (according to Rand-McNally), Vegas is home to the nation's five largest hotels and the largest freestanding neon sign. Las Vegas also has more churches per capita and the largest population of VCRs (most Vegans work in the casino industry at night and like to videotape prime-time TV programs).

And why so many churches? Residents and tourists go to the Guardian Angel church (among many others) on the Strip and pray their luck will be better the next day. For that matter, they also visit the Horseshoe Club downtown or Caesars Palace and stand in front of the $1,000,000 in cash on display at these places and pray—that some of it will become theirs.

Vegas is gaudy, with red, turquoise, and green neon shining from all sides. It's exciting. It's kitschy. And it's incredibly hot in the summertime. But it's the only amusement park adults have. And where else in the world are you going to hear Wayne Newton thanking you again and again for being a "very special audience"?

Vegas is booming. In 1987 more than 16 million people came to visit and stayed in one of the 60,000 hotel rooms available in the "Entertainment Capital of the World." Projections for the early 1990s foresee several new hotels, 20,000 additional rooms, and 20 million visitors a year.

Why so many new customers? Cheap airfares and rooms have a lot to do with it, along with the thrill available to anyone with enough money to spend. "Toke" the maître d' and bellhop correctly, spend enough money at the gaming tables, and you can be Mr. and Mrs. Las Vegas—for a couple of days.

You can also be as naughty as you want, and no one's going to yell at you for it. "Vegas is like the free square on the bingo card of life," says local comedian Pete Barbutti.

> God can't see what goes on here. When you die and go to heaven, and St. Peter checks your records, and he says, "What about the time you had the two hookers and drank the bottle of scotch and smoked the dope?" you can say, "Hey, but that was in Vegas." And St. Pete says, "Oh, yeah, that's what I did when I was there, too."

Las Vegas is a city where everyone is on a first-name basis: Sammy. Dean. Siegfried. Frank. Wayne. Engelbert. Roy. Lola. Charo. Julio. Tom. So welcome, my close personal friends, to the greatest city in the entire universe—Fabulous Las Vegas. It's a very special place, which I know you'll enjoy reading about because, hey, you are very special people.

> "Las Vegas. Trying to see all the shows in two days, staying up late, forgetting where your hotel was, where you were staying at. This is the only place in the world where you could have a good time without enjoying yourself. You're exhausted, you never sleep, everybody's searching, wandering, looking. After a while you forget what you're looking for. We'll go here, then there, we'll see that show, we saw it already, we'll see it again, then we'll sleep during the show and see the next show, then we'll go to the coffee shop, we were just in there, well let's go back in there. Then we'll go out and gamble, and we'll go and stand in the lobby and watch people for a half hour.
>
> Let's go up to the room.
> Why, what's playing up there?"
>
> —Jack Carter

ACKNOWLEDGMENTS

Las Vegas is not an easy town to photograph. Even though you'll encounter hundreds of people shooting snapshots on the street, the minute you walk into a casino with a camera around your neck the stares come fast and hard. "No photography allowed," the guard barks. The reasoning for this silly rule goes back to the old days: some guy who's fooling around with a pretty lady doesn't want damaging evidence—in the form of a photo—to get back to the wife. Additionally, gamblers can be nervous people and wouldn't want to be photographed as they play.

Luckily, in the pursuit of publicity, most hotels did open their doors and allowed me to shoot pictures—as long as my camera didn't focus on the geezer with $100,000 worth of chips under his cigar. So heartfelt thanks go to the hotel officials who let in me and my Canon—*and* my endless questions. Without answers to those questions this would be nothing but a collection of old publicity photos.

Extra special thanks go to the extra helpful hotel p.r. group: Bruce Banke, Henri Bollinger, Mary Bryant, Harvey Diedrich, Don Guglielmino, Laura Herlovich, Sharon Mason, Debbie Munch, Steve Radulovich, Jim Seagrave, Steve Schiffman, Ira David Steinberg, Denyce Tuller, Dave Verbon, and the accommodating staffs of their establishments: The Aladdin, Bally's, Binion's Horseshoe, Caesars Palace, Flamingo Hilton, Frontier, Imperial Palace, Riviera, Sahara, Stardust, Tropicana, and the Union Plaza.

"Vegas Vic" is the name of the neon cowboy downtown who waves and says "Howdy Pardner" to passers-by. Don Payne, chief of the Las Vegas News Bureau, has been saying "Howdy Pardner" to me for years and also providing lots of help. Don and his staff are responsible for the vintage photographs of Vegas that appear in this book. Thanks, Don, and, by the way, howdy.

Geno Munari showed me around town, explained the games to me, assisted me on photo shoots, and took my photograph for the jacket flap. Thanks, Geno.

Thanks also go to Pamela Allen, Donn Arden, Milton Berle, Jack and Benny Binion, Bob Boden, Bill Boyd, David Brokaw, Canon USA, David Copperfield, Sammy Davis, Jr., Sam Distefano, "Nevada" Sam Graham and Ruth, Paul and Patte Gilbert, Jimmy Grippo, Mike Hartzel, Sue Jarvis and the Special Collections department at the University of Nevada—Las Vegas, Jeff Kutash, Fluff LeCoque, Arnold Lipsman, Paul and Sue Lowden, Joyce Luman, Bill Moore, Wayne Newton, Melinda and Bonnie Saxe, Geoff Schneider, Siegfried and Roy, Webster, Steve Wynn, and Bernie Yuman.

Thank you, Tom McNamara and Jack Curry and all the great people at *USA Today*.

And, lastly, some words of appreciation to the people behind the scenes at Abbeville Press. First of all, let's start out with a man who is not only a marvelous editor, but also a close personal friend and a great humanitarian, Alan Axelrod; the finest publicist in the world, Deborah Sloan; and Mr. Marketing himself, Steven J. Pincus.

PART ONE

STORY OF A DESERT TOWN

10

CHAPTER I

A.D. 500–A.D. 1947

IN THE BEGINNING

In the beginning there were no dice or cards, no hotels or neon signs. Just the Anasazi Indians and a lot of sandy earth. The tribe lived in the Las Vegas Valley from A.D. 500 to A.D. 1150, when they left because they tired of the scalding heat.

The area was generally uninhabited for most of the time between then and the nineteenth century, although, in the late 1770s, Spanish explorers, passing through en route to New Mexico and California, dubbed the area Las Vegas, "The Meadows."

Several Americans, including the legendary trapper Jedediah Strong Smith in 1827 and explorer John C. Frémont in 1844, camped in the area on their way to other destinations. It wasn't until 1848, however, that the town took root. That was when the Treaty of Guadalupe Hidalgo was signed, ending the Mexican–American War and calling for Mexico to hand over the Nevada territory to the United States.

A couple of years later, William Bringhurst brought thirty young members of the Church of Jesus Christ of Latter-Day Saints—the Mormons—to the Las Vegas desert, following the plan set forth by Brigham Young to colonize the areas surrounding the Salt Lake Valley. Bringhurst and company built a fort and hoped the hot desert weather would encourage corn, wheat, potatoes, squash, and melons to grow; in the cold climate of northern Utah, they hadn't. But southern Nevada didn't work out, either. The heat was too strong, there wasn't enough water to support ten to twenty families, let alone thirty, and the Indians stole what crops did manage to survive. The Mormons decided to return to Salt Lake the following year.

The 1849 discovery of gold in California drew thousands to the West. In Nevada most of the activity was up north, near Reno and Virginia City, where prospectors spent many an evening drinking and gambling. But their stay was short-lived. By 1890 most of the gold had been mined out and the state quickly lost a third of its population.

RAILROADS

In 1905 the San Pedro, Los Angeles and Salt Lake Railroad established a stop in Las Vegas to serve the miners, who had come to the area when silver was discovered in small southern Nevada communities like Tonopah, Searchlight, and Ely. Within a few months, thanks to the railroad stop, Las Vegas's main street, Fremont Street, had a post office, gambling hall, bordello, bank, hotel, and saloon.

Connections were soon added to nearby Tonopah, Searchlight, Goldfield, Rhyolite, Nelson, and Goodsprings. If a miner wanted to go to these places, he had to stop in Las Vegas first. Thanks to its natural resources, the area was starting to boom, but Vegans began to feel there had to be more to life than just money. In the scorching heat of the summer, they wanted *water.*

THE DAM

In 1928, with the passage of the Boulder Canyon Project Act, Congress agreed to supply water and energy for parts of California, Nevada, and Arizona. Several places were under consideration as potential sites for the mammoth dam, including the Las Vegas vicinity. Ray Wilbur, President

Fremont Street, between First and Second, 1920s

Herbert Hoover's Secretary of the Interior, came to inspect the town. Even though garbage had been removed from the streets and the speakeasies and brothels were closed, he chose not to build the dam there. He determined that the dam should be somewhere else, and that the government could build a model city to house the construction workers and, later, the permanent personnel running the facility. He didn't want people working on the great dam to be subject to "the sins of Vegas."

"Instead of a boisterous frontier town," he declared, "it is hoped that here simple homes, gardens with fruit, and flowers, schools and playgrounds will make this a wholesome American community."

Since the dam was at first called Boulder Dam, Wilbur dubbed the new community, some twenty-five miles from Las Vegas, Boulder City, though he soon changed the name of the dam from Boulder to Hoover. Of all the communities in Nevada, it is still the only place where gambling isn't legal.

Construction on the dam began in March 1931, at a time when Vegas had just 5,165 residents. The Great Depression was under way, and work was scarce. People came from all over the country, eager for a job, although it was one of the toughest in the nation. Building the dam required moving massive amounts of earth and rock and transforming 5 million barrels of cement, 8 million tons of sand, gravel, and cobbles, 18 million pounds of structural steel, and 840 million pounds of pipe into a 726.4-foot-high, 1,244-foot-wide wall of concrete across the Colorado River. (If the concrete of the new dam had been used to build a highway, it would have stretched from Seattle to Miami.) Construction took twenty-one months, $50,000,000, and the labor of 1,200 men. No single company could handle the project, so the job was given to six firms, which teamed up as the Six Companies—W. A. Bechtel/Henry Kaiser/Warren Brothers, Utah Construction, MacDonald and Kahn, Morrison-Knudsen, the Pacific Bridge Company, and J. F. Shea.

Since the idea was to have these forces focused on their work and not on the sins of

OPPOSITE:

High scalers at work on Hoover (Boulder) Dam

BELOW:

Postcard showing stages in the construction of Hoover (Boulder) Dam

STAGES OF CONSTRUCTION IN THE BUILDING OF BOULDER DAM
ALL VIEWS TAKEN FROM THE SAME POINT, LOOKING UPSTREAM.

COMMENCEMENT OF CONSTRUCTION 1931 • FIRST CONCRETE POURING 1933 • THE DAM HALF COMPLETED 1934 • BOULDER DAM TODAY 1936

Hoover (Boulder) Dam

Vegas, the Interior Department recommended opening a commissary at the work site, and the Six Companies started paying wages in scrip to stop the workers from squandering money (and muscle) on wine, women and song (and blackjack). Las Vegas merchants were enraged, Nevada senator Tusker Oddie complained, and Interior backed off. Workers no longer had to accept payment in scrip, unless they wanted to. Most chose to take cash, which they could, indeed, spend in the wild and noisy saloons of Las Vegas.

Nearly complete on May 29, 1935, the dam was dedicated by President Franklin Delano Roosevelt on September 30, a day subsequently declared a state holiday in Arizona and Nevada. FDR also changed the name of the dam from Hoover back to Boulder; in 1947, with Roosevelt dead and buried, the 80th Congress re-renamed it Hoover Dam, its name today.

Visitors flocked to southern Nevada to see the new wonder: the largest dam in the world, half as high as New York's Empire State Building and two city blocks long; the largest man-made receptacle for water in the world—10,500 billion gallons in a reservoir 589 feet deep.

Las Vegas was no longer just a railroad stop. The tourism industry had begun. In 1939, 600,000 folks visited—compared to 500,000 that year for Yosemite and Yellowstone combined.

PHIL TOBIN

H. G. Blasdel, the governor of Nevada when the territory joined the Union in 1864, was an antigambling man. He successfully urged his territorial legislature in 1861 to pass an antigambling law—to which most law enforcement officials paid no attention; Nevadans gambled all night in saloons and mining patches. By 1869, the legislature stopped listening to the gov—and made gambling legal again (overriding Blasdel's veto). In 1909, they again outlawed wagering.

14

Thus stood the statute until 1931, when twenty-nine-year-old Winnemucca cowboy and Republican state assemblyman Phil Tobin sponsored a bill to legalize gambling as a revenue source for the state, counties, and cities, which needed new money, since mining was played out and the rest of the country was in the midst of the Depression. Besides, it was no secret that gambling was as much a part of daily life as riding a horse or sipping whiskey. "There was not a market, hotel or gas station that didn't have a slot machine or two," Tobin once told a writer, adding that law enforcement and other local officials around the state were turning their backs— usually for a price—when it came to enforcing antigambling statutes.

> The sheriff had a say in who operated a game, and determining who operated a game depended on how much money the sheriff got. . . . I didn't really give a damn about gambling and I certainly didn't know much about it, but I felt that if we legalized it, the tax revenue would be beneficial to the state.

Such a bill had failed in 1929; Tobin rewrote it and presented it again in 1931. Supporters said gambling was too widespread to ignore, and it should be taxed; opposition said gambling was a vice that would attract gangsters and bring shame upon the state. The Assembly passed the bill 24 to 11, and the Senate went for it 13 to 3.

The "wide open" gambling bill was signed into law along with another bill that liberalized wedding and divorce requirements in Nevada. All that was needed for divorce was six weeks' residency and proof of age; no blood test was required for a wedding license.

As to gambling revenues, the state charged establishments with card, craps, and roulette games $25 a month and $10 for slots. Twenty-five percent of the gaming income went to the state treasury and the other 75 percent was divided among cities and counties.

The father of Nevada gambling, rancher Phil Tobin, never gambled—except out in the fields. "The cattle business is the biggest gamble there is," said Tobin, who died in 1976 at age seventy-five. "The odds are always bad."

EARLY CASINOS

In 1931, Reno was home to the earliest gambling houses. The first *major* house was Raymond and "Pappy" Harold Smith's Harold's Club, which opened in 1935. Famous for their roadside "Harold's Club or Bust" billboards, the Smiths aimed to make gambling more accessible to the common man. Their casino was brightly lit and open to full view from the sidewalk, giving the impression that there was nothing to hide, no unsavory, smoke-filled back rooms here.

As the big Reno clubs were opening, Las Vegas was not quite a third as large as its northern neighbor. The early Vegas casinos were downtown on Fremont Street, small western-theme establishments, usually consisting of a bar, a couple of blackjack tables, a faro dealer, and a big-six wheel. The first Vegas casino license was issued to Mayme Stocker for her Northern

Fremont Street, late 1930s

15

Club, on Fremont, which she ran with her son Harold, who had won big at the roulette wheel several times in a Tijuana casino. The Northern Club would have been licensed under Harold's father's name, but he worked for the railroad, and the family figured that the railroad would not have looked favorably on an employee who ran a casino.

The success of the Northern Club brought on a wave of Fremont Street clubs, including the Apache, the first in town to feature an elevator, and the Meadows, run by Los Angeles hood Tony Cornero, who would finance the gaudy Stardust on the Strip in the 1950s.

While most newspaper space was taken up with stories of bread- and soup-lines and hard-luck poverty, editors had a welcome relief in the tourist boom of Hoover Dam and Las Vegas: "Fremont and Main are thronged with an endless procession of men in rolled-up sleeves and straw hats, civil engineers in puttees, faro dealers with their inevitable eyeshades and with gamblers," wrote the Hearst papers in 1931. "The continual sound of hammers mingles with the clink of money."

EL RANCHO VEGAS

Legal gambling was working in Nevada. Locals and tourists were spending money at the saloons, and the state was staying in business. But Vegas and Reno weren't the only games around. Yes, gambling was illegal everywhere else in the Union, but it was nevertheless quite easy to find a game in the casinos of Kentucky, Miami, Cuba, Mexico, and the coast of southern California. And gambling ships operated *legally* three miles offshore. "The boys"—a.k.a. organized crime—ran these venues—as well as nightclubs in the major cities, where there was always a game going on in the back room. Certainly, it was more comfortable to place a wager in a legal establishment. But the people with the big bucks, the high-society set that visited the clubs of New York and Chicago, weren't going to travel to Vegas to gamble in a "sawdust joint"—which is what the new clubs were: western saloons, in which cowboys sporting ten-gallon hats drank whiskey and played old-time card games.

The first operation to begin to break out of this mold, the first that was a "gaming resort" as opposed to a small bar with a game room, was El Rancho Vegas, built in 1941 on dusty Highway 91, the road to Los Angeles. Today that road is Las Vegas Boulevard, better known as "The Strip."

El Rancho was a sprawling wagon-train ring of one-story cabanas, several miles south of

El Rancho Vegas, the first Strip resort

16

the knot of small hotels and gambling joints downtown. It stood alone in the dirt, in the midst of nothing but isolation.

And how did owner Tommy Hull decide to build his establishment in such a place? The story goes that Hull, a hotelier who had built El Ranchos in Sacramento and Fresno, California, had a flat tire on Highway 91 one hot afternoon. As he sat by the side of the road in the scorching sun watching the stream of traffic zoom by, he was visited by inspiration: What a great place for a hotel!

It was risky, building a place three miles from the center of town, but Hull figured that with gambling, fun, and sun as his calling cards, the Boulder Dam tourists would stop by for a visit.

The motif of El Rancho—which opened on April 3, 1941—was western, its architecture Yosemite cabin-style, rustic and friendly, sort of a dude ranch. Everyone wore western outfits, locals felt comfortable, and tourists relaxed in the cabins away from the city.

Hull remained in Los Angeles, although he commuted to Vegas often. Because El Rancho appealed to locals, rather than the gamblers of New York and Los Angeles, he was never able to make much of a success of the place. He sold it in 1947 to Beldon Kattleman, who added big-name stars to the show room and really started doing business.

THE LAST FRONTIER

The Last Frontier was Vegas's second Strip resort. R. E. Griffith, who ran movie theaters and hotels in Texas and New Mexico, financed the place, putting nephew William J. Moore in charge of construction. It opened eighteen months after El Rancho, on October 30, 1942. Moore had built an El Rancho hotel/theater for Griffith in Deming, New Mexico, but they couldn't use that name here. The new moniker reflected Griffith's notion that Vegas was the last frontier, where freedom and the western spirit abounded; the Frontier's motto: "The Modern West in Old Splendor."

Gambling could be had here, of course, but the Frontier, like El Rancho, was mainly a dude ranch, a place for people to spend a week, lie in the sun, go swimming, ride horses, and gamble—a little bit.

They could also eat well. In the Frontier's Ramona Room guests could order "juicy rich prime ribs of Eastern steer beef, cooked in rock salt, served from the cart at your table with Idaho baked potato with chives, tossed green salad, rolls and coffee" for the 1942 price of $1.50.

Moore gathered authentic pioneer-day furnishings from all over the West—but construction

The Last Frontier, Vegas's second Strip resort

17

Bugsy Siegel and his Fabulous
Flamingo

wasn't an easy task. World War II made materials scarce, so Griffith imported them from downtown clubs. He bought a grand, forty-foot bar with French beveled glass from Fremont Street's Arizona Club.

Griffith died a year after the place opened, and Moore took over, selling out in 1951 to gambler Jake Kozloff, who changed the name in 1955 because he felt Vegas was no longer the *last*, but now the *New* Frontier. He equipped the joint with "ultra-modern furnishings" and changed the slogan to "Out of This World." In 1967, following further renovation, it became known simply as The Frontier.

BUGSY SIEGEL AND HIS FABULOUS FLAMINGO

Las Vegas will be proud of the Flamingo. It will become one of the world's greatest playgrounds. Nothing has been spared to make the Flamingo one of the most glamorous and comfortable places of entertainment in the entire world. The Flamingo is for the people of Las Vegas as well as visitors from anywhere. The Flamingo cuisine will be the finest that money can buy and brains can serve, prepared by a kitchen crew gathered from all parts of the world.
—*Bugsy Siegel in a 1946 newspaper ad announcing the opening of the Flamingo Hotel*

If El Rancho and the Last Frontier were there first, why do people always assume that Benjamin "Bugsy" Siegel's Fabulous Flamingo was the first Vegas Strip resort?

Because El Rancho and the Frontier were essentially dude ranches, western hotels that happened to harbor some gambling. Siegel realized that he had to offer more than tables and slots to get the gamblers away from Reno. He had to have the finest entertainment, hotel, and grounds in the world. The Flamingo was the first opulent showplace in Vegas, its design influenced by the classy Miami hotels, appealing to swingers and people with money—not the local cowboys. Siegel's vision of Vegas—the twenty-four-hour town without clocks, but with plenty of women, booze, and gambling, the playground of the West—was incarnated in the hotel. Both Griffith's version and the western image Hull was trying to establish vanished.

Before heading west, Siegel had been the partner of notorious mobster Meyer Lansky (they were the Bugs and Meyer Gang of New York), but he left for greener pastures, specifically California, where he controlled gambling.

A handsome dude with movie-star good looks, Siegel dressed sharp in pin-striped suits, fedora hats, and monogrammed silk shirts, just like gangsters in the movies. Hollywood friends included Jean Harlow (a frequent date) and George Raft, who, of course, often played gangsters. "I never called him Bugsy," Raft once told an interviewer. "He hated it, and nobody in his right mind ever called him that to his face. The mob called him Bugs because he was hotheaded, and it stuck."

Siegel explained why he came to Las Vegas in a rare 1947 interview with gambling author John Scarne:

I had a little trouble with [California] Governor Earl Warren. I owned a piece of all those gambling ships that were getting plenty of action three miles off the coast of southern California. Business was so good we had plans to add a dozen more boats. And just when I thought I had it made, Governor Warren came along and closed gambling up tight as a drum, not only in the state but on the boats, too. Overnight, my dream of a Monte Carlo in the ocean is killed.

So I'm thinking about where I can find another spot away from any other casinos—a place like the ocean so that when people come to gamble they can't go any place else but have to stick with me. There were too many sawdust joints in Vegas, Reno and other Nevada towns, but I figured it this way. If people will take a trip out into the ocean to gamble, they'll go to a desert, too—especially if it's legal and they don't have to worry about being pinched. So one day I drive into Nevada looking for a nice desert spot and I picked this one because the price was right and

The 1950s-era Flamingo

it's on the main road to L.A. Then I took a trip around the country and tried to interest some of the boys in the proposition. Some of them thought I was nuts. But I dug up the dough, and here I am with a $5,000,000 hotel and a casino full of customers.

What you see here today is nothing. More and more people are moving to California every day, and they love to gamble. Since it's legal here in the desert, and not very far away, they'll come here. In ten years this'll be the biggest gambling center in the world.

The Vegas city fathers were uncomfortable about giving a gaming license to a known criminal, but they figured that since Siegel was already entrenched as overlord of the local race-betting biz, he would be in de facto charge of the gambling houses anyway. They considered it more desirable to let Siegel operate openly on a promise to behave than to turn him down and have him run it undercover with an associate as his front.

Gambling was a great investment for Bugsy and the boys—especially since, at the time, Nevada's gaming regulations operated under the honor system. Siegel was asked to count his winnings and pay taxes based on a percentage of that count. It was easy enough to "skim" a portion of the winnings from the unreported figures and pocket it. The ease of pulling off the skim enticed other mobsters to Vegas.

Siegel got most of the financing for the hotel from Lansky and the boys back East, but it wasn't easy getting supplies in the closing days of the war, and construction of the Flamingo took much longer than expected. The hotel still wasn't finished on December 26, 1946, when Siegel decided to open anyway and bring some revenue in. Jimmy Durante, Xavier Cugat, and Rose Marie provided the entertainment on opening night; guests marveled at the full-grown palm trees and live flamingos that were imported from Florida for the opening. Grass was planted around the entire area—which eight months earlier had been desert. Siegel's hotel was named after his red-haired doll, Virginia Hill, whom he called "The Flamingo." She wore a $3,500 orange-red gown created for the opening; it was called—what else?—"The Flamingo."

Siegel's new playground, wrote Bob Thomas for the Associated Press, "looks like a set MGM wanted to build but couldn't because of budget limitations."

But all was not well. There were more winners than losers; the Flamingo lost $300,000 the first week. Siegel switched dice, changed cards, mixed dealers, but to no avail. There wasn't anything to skim when more money went out than came in.

Bugsy decided to close down after two weeks and reopen only after the hotel was finished. That was in March; the hotel lost money for three weeks in a row. By May, the casino finally went into the black, but the boys back East were restless. They wanted their loans repaid. They were convinced that the Flamingo was actually making lots of money—but that Siegel wasn't giving them all the facts.

On June 20, 1947, Siegel decided to get away for a while from the pressures of running the hotel and went to Beverly Hills to spend time at Virginia Hill's house. It was there, while reading the *Los Angeles Times* in an easy chair in front of the window, that he was gunned down. The assassination was strategically staged outside of Las Vegas, since a murder in town would have been bad publicity.

In fact, the rub-out turned out to be great publicity, capturing headlines in every major newspaper in the country. "Everyone wanted to see the place that Benny Siegel built," says Hank Greenspun, the editor-publisher of the *Las Vegas Sun* who served as the Flamingo's publicist back in the beginning. "He came up the hard way, as a hoodlum on the streets of New York, but he was accepted by the movie crowd in Hollywood and wanted to move up in life," says Greenspun of Siegel. "He figured the only way would be to build a monument so people would say that's the place Benny Siegel built. It was his way of gaining respect."

In literature and the movies, Bugsy Siegel lives on. He was "Moe Green," the New York gangster who started Las Vegas in *The Godfather,* and he was a character in Harold Robbins's *79 Park Avenue.* But there is no Bugsy Siegel Street in Vegas, nor any statue in the town square. (Of course, there is no town square, either.) The Flamingo Hilton (as it is now called) plays down the role of its famous founder, but Bugsy's own "Presidential Suite," a $300-a-day fourth-story pad, has been preserved in all the glory of its original green decor, with 1950s-style palm tree wallpaper, a pool table in the middle, mid-century literature on the bookshelves. The suite overlooks the pool, near which is a plaque identifying "Bugsy's Rose Garden" and honoring the Flamingo's founder for being an accomplished gardener—albeit "better known for having blood on his hands rather than topsoil."

"I just met a man who isn't building a hotel."

—Joe E. Lewis

CHAPTER 2
Blasts and Boom

THE D.I.

"The boys" installed new management—Arizona bookie Gus Greenbaum—at the Flamingo, which was renovated with a million dollars borrowed from Chicago's Capone gang. With all this and in the wake of publicity following the Siegel rub-out, the Flamingo thrived; the boys back East liked the return they were getting and decided to come out for more. The Thunderbird, funded by Meyer Lansky's brother Jake, was the Strip follow-up to the Flamingo. Then came the swanky Desert Inn, financed by the Cleveland gang—former bootleggers who ran a luxurious casino in Covington, Kentucky, near Cincinnati. The D.I. was billed as the gambler's gambling house.

"These guys were gambling people," says Mort Saiger, who worked at the Desert Inn—the D.I.—as a dealer during the '50s, after a long stint at the Last Frontier.

> They attracted a different type of clientele. It was a different type of gambling. By that I mean it was on a larger scale. There was no such thing as $100 maximum. If you wanted to bet $200, $300, $400, or $500—fine, go ahead.
>
> The Frontier was on a much smaller scale. Mr. Griffith was a theater man, not a gambling man. At the D.I., you came into the lobby, you fell right into the casino. As a matter of fact, you had to look for the registration desk, where at the Frontier you came in and you had to look for the casino.

A former San Diego bellhop and downtown casino operator, Wilbur Clark, started building the D.I.; when he ran out of funds, he went to the Cleveland boys—Moe Dalitz, Morris Kleinman, Lou and Bernie Rothkopf—for financial assistance. They agreed to call the place Wilbur Clark's Desert Inn, and they agreed that the boys would run the show and Clark would front it.

When Edgar Bergen and Charlie McCarthy, singer Vivian Blaine, and Donn Arden's showgirls and boys opened the D.I.'s Painted Desert Room on April 24, 1950, the casino was packed. "It was like carnival night," recalls Frank Sennes, who was the D.I.'s entertainment director. "Women were all dressed up in their minks . . . and the men were wearing tuxes. They did so well on the first night that they paid for the entire place in one night." The D.I. had cost $1,500,000 to build.

Instead of the traditional western or Miami themes, the D.I. was desert-oriented on the outside—its trademark a painted desert scene highlighted by a Joshua tree—but on the inside it was a high-class eastern establishment, offering eastern nightclub fare, to boot.

"We were the hottest thing in town because we were the first eastern line [of dancers]," says former D.I. showgirl Jeanie Malone.

> Up until that time all of the girls had been local dancers. Donn's qualifications were very rigid, he wanted [the girls] to be good looking; you didn't necessarily have to be a great dancer—because he could *make* you look great—but you had to be a lady, and you had to dress well.

23

Wilbur Clark and his Desert Inn. Clark was the frontman for the hotel, which was run by "the boys" from Cleveland.

OPPOSITE:
Opening night at the Desert Inn casino

When Donn Arden, who had been working for the Cleveland boys in some of their eastern nightclubs, was asked to put on a show in Vegas, he felt "obliged to go. They were the boys and they paid well." They also believed in spending money on girls and beautiful costumes. "I wouldn't dare use a bunny suit for a costume," Arden says. "It had to be real ermine. I wouldn't dare go to a Lerner's shoe shop and buy shoes. Oh no, the shoes had to be custom made by David Evins and all of this sort of thing, which I loved."

With the new money coming into town, Sennes was able to hire many of Hollywood's top talents for Las Vegas debuts: Frank Sinatra, Danny Kaye, Noël Coward. The D.I. was *the* hot club in Vegas for much of the 1950s. But the sailing wasn't all smooth, as the federal government started getting uptight about known hoods moving into Las Vegas, setting up shop—and then becoming model citizens.

THE KEFAUVER COMMISSION

"Big time gambling is amoral," said Senator Estes Kefauver, who in 1950 formed the Committee to Investigate Organized Crime in Interstate Commerce. "I refer to the casino type of operation, which is more often crooked than not. Gambling produces nothing and adds nothing to the economy or society of our nation."

"The Kefauver Commission" was investigating the role of organized crime in America and taking a particularly hard look at the mob's role in gambling. "Both morally and financially, legalized gambling in Nevada is a failure," said Kefauver after the hearings were concluded in 1951.

It is true that revenue derived from state and local levies on the gambling dives is welcome . . . however, the amount the state receives is only a pitiful fraction of the millions of dollars themselves drained from the pockets of the public.

Kefauver's view was shared by many other lawmakers. Congress had tried many times to outlaw gambling everywhere in America, but Nevada's Senator Pat McCarran, head of the Judiciary Committee, was always able to block such bills by mustering the forces of southern senators, who received in return McCarran's support against civil rights issues.

After the commission publicized the fact that illegal gambling houses were operating throughout the country and that corrupt officials were in cahoots with gaming operators, plush underground casinos in places like Florida and Kentucky were forced to close. But by exposing the illegal casinos, Senator Kefauver actually helped Las Vegas by shutting down the competition, which sent gamblers—and bosses—to a place where gaming was legal. Benny Binion from Texas, the Cleveland gang, and bookie Gus Greenbaum from Phoenix (who ran the Flamingo) had invested prior to the Kefauver Commission findings, so Vegas would have continued to attract out-of-state gambling money even if Kefauver's committee had never existed. But it is a fact that ten hotel/casinos were built between 1951 and 1955 through partial funding from illegal outside operations forced to liquidate.

One gambler told gaming author John Scarne in the 1950s: "I love that man Kefauver. When he drove me out of an illegal casino operation in Florida and into a legalized operation in Nevada, he made me a respectable law-abiding citizen and a millionaire."

How did the Las Vegas publicity machine deal with the national media's focus on the relationship between crime and gambling? By dishing out the likes of this:

Las Vegas has a sense of freedom and exhilaration that's contagious. You'll find open-hearted hospitality, old-fashioned friendship and rip-snorting frontier freedom. Your enjoyment will be limited only by your capacity to enjoy. The gates swing wide for you, the hand is extended, the music is playing . . . light and set stranger, because chuck's on.

ATOM BLASTS

Your typical 1950s desert atom blast, in living color

"A thrill for visitors," said the announcer for a Vegas Chamber of Commerce promotional film about the city. "Watch closely for a man-made sun, in the western wonderland of daytime sun and nighttime fun."

At a time when futuristic movies like *The Day the Earth Stood Still* were playing at the Bijou, when space exploration was on the tips of many tongues, the Vegas P.R. experts successfully turned a potential disaster into free positive publicity. The A-bomb—capable of blowing up the entire state of Nevada—was the greatest publicity stunt Vegas had ever had: just good, clean American fun in the dazzling sun. Las Vegas "is like one big Fourth of July picnic—with fireworks courtesy of the Atomic Energy Commission (AEC)," wrote the *New York Times*, adding that the A-bombs were providing "the greatest tourist lure since the invention of nickel slot machines." Vegas flacks promoted the "Atomic Hairdo" (your basic beehive) and told of the "Atomic Cocktail" (vodka, brandy, champagne, and a dash of sherry) served at the Desert Inn. Cheesecake

1950s Las Vegas skyline: that cloud in the picture is an atom bomb blast.

photos of showgirls in "Atomic" swimsuits were sent regularly to newspaper and magazine editors.

Atomic bomb tests began during the Korean War. In December 1950, the virtually uninhabited desert area of Nye County, some sixty-five miles northwest of Las Vegas and eighty-five miles south of Tonopah, was chosen by the AEC as the site of "relatively low-yield nuclear detonations." Officials said the site offered low population density, good weather conditions, government-owned land, access to labor and supplies, and security.

The first blast—code named "Buster Jangle"—went off on January 27, 1951, and was quickly followed by four more within a month. Once the photos of Fremont Street with a mushroom-cloud backdrop started appearing in newspapers and magazines, tourists began arriving from all over the country to watch the historic explosions. Reporters had a field day writing about how gamblers responded to the free outside entertainment. Wrote Bob Considine for the Associated Press:

> The players . . . really don't mind. It's doubtful if any of them, especially those who are winning good or badly stuck, would notice the A-bomb if the AEC boys touched off one in Bugsy Siegel's old chartreuse suite in the plushy Flamingo. There are too many important things on their minds to worry about that kind of inconsequential horseplay.

A Las Vegas Sears salesman told *The New Yorker* magazine in 1952 that an elderly lady from Los Angeles pulled up to the store one day, bought some shirts, and asked him to ring them up in a hurry because her husband was waiting in the car. "She said she wanted to hand the shirts down to her grandsons as heirlooms that had come from Las Vegas just before it was wiped off the face of the earth." The Desert Inn's Wilbur Clark told the magazine:

> I don't know exactly how much the bomb had to do with it, but around shot time the play in our casino seemed to go up and the drinking got heavier. The curious thing was that guests would drive here from L.A. to see a shot and then not bother to look at it. I'd instruct my pitmen to let the players at their tables know when it was about time for the flash, but the players would go right on with their games.

Gamblers haven't even bothered looking out the window since 1963. The Limited Test Ban treaty signed with the Soviets that year restricted testing to underground blasts.

ANOTHER BOOM

Seventy miles southwest of the AEC site, "the boys" were involved in many above-ground tests themselves. The object: to see how many grand hotel/casinos could be built and continue to do business. Here are the results of the 1950s building boom:

Cheesecake in the Atomic Age

29

The Sahara, 1950s

The Sahara

Milton Prell, a gaming operator from Butte, Montana, had a concept that wasn't influenced by Miami, the desert, or the Old West. His idea was Africa, Vegas-style. He called his playground the Sahara, "Jewel of the Desert." In front of the building Prell erected a desert scene depicting a nomadic caravan, complete with Saharan camels. Inside the hotel were life-size models of African warriors, spears held high, standing guard in front of the Congo Room, where the stars performed.

The Sahara had begun its existence back in July 1947 as the Bingo Club, a small three-hundred-seat bingo parlor directly across the street from El Rancho. Prell bought the place, changed the concept and name, built a hotel, and opened for business in October 1952 with 240 rooms and singer-dancer Ray Bolger in the showroom. Financing came from Dallas real estate magnate A. Pollard Simon and builder Del Webb, who in lieu of payment for his services took a 20 percent interest in the Hotel Sahara.

In 1958, the Sahara was notable for being the first gaming establishment to obtain funding from an actual bank. The Bank of Las Vegas (now called Valley National), run by E. Parry Thomas, made a $1,000,000 loan to the Sahara to build two hundred rooms. "Prior to that, we had borrowed money from groups of people that would bank together, and we paid as much as 19 percent interest to them," says Sam Boyd, casino manager at the Sahara during the 1950s. "In some instances you had to give a piece of your business away to borrow the money to go on."

The Sands

Texas gambler Jake Freedman came to Vegas from Houston, hoping to build a "Holiday Inn." His idea and name for it—which predate the Holiday Inn motel chain Kemmons Wilson started in Memphis in 1958—were inspired by the 1942 Bing-Crosby–Danny Kaye movie *Holiday Inn*.

Freedman found partners in Jack Entratter and Carl Cohen of the New York Copacabana, reputed fronts for "the boys" from New York, but government building restrictions prohibited new construction at the time, so Freedman had to remodel the old La Rue restaurant, in spring 1952.

30

Opening night at the Sands

Postcard: "On the fabulous 'Strip' in Las Vegas, THE SANDS stands out as the most magnificent of resort hotels . . ."

When a construction worker asked Freedman what he wanted to call his new palace, he replied: "There's so much sand in this damned place that my socks are full of it. So why don't we call it 'The Sand' until it's finished. Then we'll call it the Holiday Inn." The worker pointed out that "The Sand" didn't have much of a ring to it; "The Sands," he said, "would sound much better." And the place never was called the Holiday Inn.

The Sands, whose motto was "Fun in the Sun," had two hundred rooms in five two-story Bermuda-modern-style buildings, each named after a racetrack. A circular seventeen-story tower with 777 rooms was added in 1965.

The hotel was *the* Vegas hotel of the 1950s. No overall theme, except for high-society sun-worshipping by day and swinging by night. Sinatra was the main star, and the Sands was as hip as they get, the song "Come Fly with Me" setting the tone.

Danny Thomas and the "Copa Girls"—"The Most Beautiful Girls in the World"—opened on December 15, 1952, followed by performers like Milton Berle, Sinatra, Nat "King" Cole, and Sammy Davis, Jr.

Entratter, a former bouncer at the Copa, was revered by show biz performers. He was the first of the Vegas impresarios to understand that "superstars" in a show room meant full houses, which in turn meant packed casinos before and after the show. He also understood that

The ultimate 1950s Vegas publicity shot: a floating crap game at the Sands

Mr. Sinbad, as he looked back in 1954 atop the Dunes Hotel

performers wanted to be treated like royalty, that they needed to be wined and dined and taken care of. Entratter did that, and the biggest stars of the 1950s and early 1960s all played the Sands.

The Dunes

What set "The Miracle in the Desert" apart from the Sahara—the "Desert Jewel"—was its Arabian as opposed to North African theme. There was a ninety-foot swimming pool, palm trees all around, 194 rooms, and a 30-foot-high sultan effigy atop the building. He was named Mr. Sinbad.

Financed by the Teamsters Pension Fund for the New England "boys," the Dunes opened with a *Magic Carpet Revue* featuring Hollywood musical star Vera-Ellen. But the Dunes found that there wasn't enough business to go around. As the Royal Nevada and Riviera also were to discover, the Dunes learned that the pie could only be sliced in so many ways. In 1954 the management of the Sands took over the Dunes for a while and tried to turn it around with some high-profile visits by Frank Sinatra. No dice. The hotel/casino went bankrupt and became a motel, until Major (his name, not rank) Riddle, owner of a Chicago trucking company and a loyal Teamster associate, came to the rescue in 1957. His formula for solvency? Stripping on the Strip.

Riddle hired Lou Costello (of Abbott and Costello) to star in a version of "Minsky's Follies" for two months at the beginning of the year. It was the first Vegas show to feature nudes on stage—although their nipples were covered with pasties and tassles. The show was a smash, returned six months later, and stayed for four and a half years. With bumps and grinds in the show room, gamblers were more than happy to drop money at the Dunes's craps tables.

33

The Riviera in 1953, the first Vegas high-rise

The Riviera

While the Riviera suffered from the same problem the Dunes had—business spread too thin—it did look quite different from the other Strip resorts. Funded by "the boys" of Miami, the Riviera went one step further than the Flamingo in presenting a clone of the grand Miami resort in Las Vegas. An orange, L-shaped, nine-story, two-hundred-fifty-room building, the Riv was a radical departure from the one- and two-story ranch-style hotels that had preceded it. It was the first Vegas high-rise.

The builders were the same men who had built the famous Fontainebleu and Eden Roc hotels in Miami; their aim was to capture the coastal and tropical feeling of the French Riviera in a city where Lake Mead offered the only coastline—and that was totally man-made. No attempt was made to recreate the Atlantic Ocean in the lobby, but the owners did name each floor after familiar French Riviera locales such as Cannes, Nice, and Monte Carlo.

To lure the gamblers in, the Riv opened in 1953 with the hottest star of the moment, Liberace, who was paid the then unheard of salary of $50,000 a week to leave the Last Frontier. It was the most money anyone had ever received for performing in a Vegas club. This salary precedent "killed show biz in the nightclubs all over the country," according to Frank Sennes, entertainment director at the Stardust and Desert Inn in the 1950s.

There was no way the Copa in New York or Chez Paree in Chicago could afford to pay anywhere near that kind of money. Once salaries started to escalate, the

34

The Fremont: in 1956, the tallest building in Nevada

entertainers were making so much more money in Vegas that they didn't want to work for less in the other clubs.

And the expense was to no avail. The Riviera was heading for financial trouble.

The Chicago mob took over the casino in 1956 and installed Gus Greenbaum—formerly of the Flamingo—to run gambling operations. The Greenbaum magic worked again; like the Flamingo, the Riviera started turning a profit.

Unfortunately for Greenbaum, he had a nasty heroin habit; he started sending less cash back home to the boys, and they weren't too happy about that. During a 1958 Thanksgiving visit to Phoenix, Greenbaum and his wife were found in a hotel room with their throats slashed.

The Fremont

Throughout the 1950s, the Strip had always been home to "carpet joints"—establishments where the better class of people gambled, in contrast to the "sawdust joints," small gambling halls with Wild West themes, some gaming tables, and dirty floors, all located downtown on Fremont Street. Then, in 1956, the Fremont Hotel opened its doors. At the time the fifteen-story hotel/casino was the tallest building in the state, its roof providing great views of the atomic tests.

Financed by the Florida "boys" and gambler Ed Levinson, the Fremont was a lot more than a storefront with three or four blackjack tables, a craps table, and a roulette wheel; it was a hotel with 160 rooms and a swimming pool. And it featured entertainment, too. The most

Young Wayne Newton playing a Vegas show room

famous entertainers at the Fremont were the Newton Brothers—Wayne and Jerry—who reigned for five years in the Carnival Room lounge. The brothers had to be escorted into the lounge because they were underage. When the lounge closed in 1966, the pair went their separate ways; Wayne moved to the Strip, where he's been playing ever since.

The Stardust

Los Angeles gangster Tony Cornero, who operated the *S.S. Rex* gambling ship off the Santa Monica coast in the 1930s and 1940s, had been a downtown Vegas gaming operator in the late 1940s and early '50s. But his dream was to build a large, classy Strip hotel. When it opened in 1958, one critic said the Stardust looked like the wildest dreams of Salvador Dalí. The outside was an astronomer's nightmare, decorated by a model of the earth turning in a welter of flashing planets, comets, and meteors.

Cornero's hotel was typical Vegas overkill: the largest casino (In The World); the longest pool (In The World), the greatest number of rooms (1,100—if not the most in the world, certainly the most in Vegas), the greatest supper club (anywhere), and the brightest and largest neon sign in Las Vegas: 7,100 feet of neon tubing and 11,000 incandescent lamps along the 216-foot front of the hotel. The glow was visible three miles away. But Cornero never lived to see his Stardust sign shine. One morning, shooting craps at the Desert Inn, he gasped for air and fell to the floor. Heart attack. Died with his dice in his hands.

Moe Dalitz and Morris Kleinman of the Desert Inn bought the Stardust and ran it in tandem with the D.I. across the street. The D.I.'s resident floor-show producer, Donn Arden, brought to the Stardust an import of his own French show, *Lido de Paris*, the first 100 percent topless show in a Vegas show room. Featured were a Parisian street scene, fireworks over the Eiffel Tower, a dam bursting, and lots of topless showgirls. Vegas audiences had never seen anything like it.

"The show was magical," says Corinne Entratter, a former Sands—"covered"—showgirl who attended opening night.

> God, I was kind of shocked to see women walk across the stage, nude, with their breasts hanging out, but actually it was beautiful. It was like looking at a nude in a painting. That isn't shocking. It was really like a painting coming to life.

36

"Minsky's was the first topless show in Las Vegas, but that was burlesque, and there's a difference," says Arden.

You grind, you twirl the tassles, you have a firecracker stuck up the ass. It's a real striptease. I didn't bring striptease to America. I brought beautiful nudes done in a classy, elegant way. The Minsky's shows were raucous and bawdy. My shows didn't work that way. They had a touch of class.

The *Las Vegas Review-Journal* didn't agree.

The people of the state of Nevada may be liberal, but they also have a high standard of morals. . . . If the operators of the strip hotels who revel in the indecency of their stage shows believe that all sense of value among Nevadans is dead, then they should take a look at their hole card.

But bare breasts on the Strip brought in the folks. The Thunderbird followed with the *Ecstasy on Ice* skating show; the New Frontier's *Holiday in Japan* featured Oriental nudes; and the *Folies Bergère* at the Tropicana featured nude showgirls.

Bishop Dwyer of the Archdiocese of Nevada issued an edict telling all Catholics to stay away. A ban-the-nudes bill passed the state Senate in 1959 but floundered in the Assembly.

"When it comes to gambling, I only gamble for laughs. In fact, last week I laughed away my car."

—Milton Berle

The 1950s Stardust, which one critic said looked "like the wildest dreams of Salvador Dalí"

OVERLEAF:
Lido de Paris, the longest-running show in Vegas history, during its opening week in June 1958

BLACK IN VEGAS

Sammy Davis, Jr., has been performing in Las Vegas ever since 1945, when he, his father, and his uncle—The Will Mastin Trio—opened for Johnny O'Brian, the Irish tenor, and the El Rancho Adorables at El Rancho Vegas. No performer has been playing the city as long. No white performer has suffered the indignities Davis endured playing Vegas in the 1940s and 1950s.

"We were performing at the hotel, but we couldn't stay there," says Davis. "We couldn't eat there. We couldn't gamble in the casino. We couldn't walk in the front door."

Other black performers in Vegas, like Nat "King" Cole, Lena Horne, Pearl Bailey, Billy Eckstine, Ella Fitzgerald, and Harry Belafonte, were treated similarly.

Even though he was starring on the Strip, Davis never even attempted to get into a show room to see his fellow black performers. "Not a chance. You wouldn't dare. There was no one I wanted to see, anyway."

No one?

"All the performers stayed at the same rooming house on the West Side. We'd perform for ourselves after the show. We'd sing all night."

The Will Mastin Trio, Nat Cole, Lena Horne—they all had to sleep, eat, and entertain themselves on the west side of town—the black ghetto. Even though their performances were bringing dollars into the white casinos, they were treated like servants.

"In the Monte Carlo of North America, the Negro [which represented 10 percent of the Vegas populace at the time] finds little welcome anywhere," wrote *Ebony* in 1951.

He is barred from practically every place whites go for entertainment or services. Whenever a Negro is spotted in

a gambling hall, it is safe to wager that he is behind a broom, mop, or dishcloth.

Local NAACP president Lubertha Warden told the magazine that Las Vegas

lags far behind all cities in the West in civil rights with exception of the deep South. . . . [Blacks,] no matter how intelligent, or well-dressed, cannot enter most of the licensed establishments in the city, or must accept inferior Jim Crow services.

Even back in the beginning, the "Six Companies" had refused to hire blacks for work at Hoover Dam. After prodding by the NAACP, they relented and hired ten blacks, who were forced to live in separate quarters from the whites.

In the South, blacks could go to the back door and be served. In Vegas, there was no back-door policy; they just weren't served at all. And no place was more antiblack than the big casinos on the Strip.

"Can you imagine that in those days Harry Belafonte [who was making $20,000 a week to play Vegas] wasn't allowed in any of the casinos or restaurants?" asks Vegas producer Bill Moore. "The girls of the line were told that if they talked to Harry, or if they were seen with him, they would be fired."

"What they said was that they didn't want to offend the Texans," recalls Davis. "'Black and white people just don't gamble together, dig?' 'We don't want no niggers around the crap table.'"

What you've got to remember is that Vegas was built upon Texas gamblers' money. That's why you had a guy like Jakie Freedman at the Sands walking around with his big cowboy hat; they had the Texas Copa Girls on their line. When you've got a situation like that, "the boys" aren't about to make too many policy announcements. "What we do back East is back East, but this is their world—we're just trying to make an inroad."

Throughout most of the 1950s, the most black performers like Davis could hope for in the way of watching a show was to "maybe go backstage and stand in the wings." As the decade came to a close, race relations in Vegas started slowly to get better.

When Davis began working the Sands in 1958, he went to hotel entertainment chief Jack Entratter and complained that friends from California wanted to come see his show. "What am I supposed to tell them?" Davis asked.

Entratter promised to let them in the show room.

It just started getting broken down in bits and pieces. Young guys like myself started coming in. I was really bodacious. I was there when it was happening for me professionally.

Sammy Davis, Jr., with the other two-thirds of the Will Mastin Trio—Mastin and Davis, Sr. They were welcome on any Vegas stage—just stay out of the casinos.

When we moved from the Last Frontier to the Sands, I told Jack [Entratter] that I had to live there, too. I told him I couldn't work where I don't live; it didn't make any sense. "You know how in the old days I lived in Harlem, Jack. Now when I work in the Copa I stay downtown."

Entratter allowed Davis, his dad, and uncle to live at the Sands. But they were about the only blacks afforded that opportunity.

By 1961, a year after the filming of *Ocean's 11* at the Sands, blacks were still having a hard time getting in the front door of the hotel. Davis was sitting with Frank Sinatra in the lobby one afternoon when a black couple walked in the front door and two security guards walked over to block them—"not from coming to our table," Davis explains, "but from coming into the Sands hotel."

Davis and Sinatra walked over to the guards and Sinatra asked them what the problem was, and they said (Davis recalls), " 'We've got rules, Mr. Sinatra.' " The unofficial president of the hotel told the guards that the couple were his guests and ushered them in. Then Sinatra called Sands executive Carl Cohen on the phone and (according to Davis) said, " 'This shit's gotta stop and it's gotta stop now. We don't believe in that kind of shit, and if any of the people in this joint feel differently, tell them to come see me.' "

"And that," Davis says, "was it."

The next day Davis went to see Entratter and suggested that now was the time to start hiring blacks at the Sands. " 'I agree with you, Sam, it's time, but where am I going to find them?' " Davis recalls Entratter's reply.

The entertainer went to the NAACP, which sent over a group of applicants; suddenly, the Sands was hiring black bellhops, busboys, and waiters. "And from that moment," says Davis, "the door just started swinging open."

Sammy Davis, Jr., moved to the Desert Inn in 1967—among the last Vegas resorts to open the doors to blacks. Davis was playing there at the time that Howard Hughes owned the place;

Lounge legend Shecky Greene

Hughes's feelings about blacks were not friendly. He wrote in a memo to an aide:

> I can summarize my attitude about employing more Negroes very simply—I think it is a wonderful idea for somebody, somewhere else. I feel Negroes have already made enough progress to last the next 100 years and there is such a thing as overdoing it.

So each night Davis used to do a joke about how the D.I. had given him a membership in their golf club, but had strange hours for him to play—like 9 P.M. Sinatra would call him and say he was overstepping the boundaries—he should cool it with the jokes. "But I did it anyway. And the doors finally swung open."

"It was very unfair," says performer Morey Amsterdam, "but that's the way it was in those days. We were not protesters. It was a place to work. You went in and did your job and kept your mouth shut."

"It was a crime," says comedian Shecky Greene.

> A lot of the owners of the clubs were Jewish. I used to do a routine about all the Jews that owned the hotels. My people have wandered for centuries and centuries and they ended up right back in the desert. What's frightening is that we didn't do something as a collective group of entertainers. We didn't all collectively say we refuse to work until . . . We just totally accepted that this was the way things was. No black dealers. No black pit bosses. It's frightening to think that existed in the West.

"Now," says Davis, "when I see black people walking down the street in Vegas, I just sit back and smile."

Harry Belafonte: big in Vegas—but he couldn't get into the casinos either

CHAPTER 3
Mobsters and Moguls

THE TEAMSTERS

In Las Vegas, Bugsy Siegel may have been the great innovator, but Jimmy Hoffa was the big investor. His Teamsters Central States Pension Fund poured some $269,000,000 into several Vegas casinos—the Dunes, Sahara, Caesars, Circus Circus, Fremont, Stardust, Desert Inn, Four Queens, Aladdin, Landmark, Sands, and Riviera, which turned to the Teamsters for help because traditional banking was wary of investing in the gaming industry. By 1974 the fund held 56.1 percent of all loans to Clark County (the county that encompasses Las Vegas).

Hoffa was bullish on Vegas. At one point in 1955 he recommended to the pension fund board a $10,000,000 purchase of the Sands, but was rebuffed; his associates thought it too risky a venture. Instead, Hoffa and the fund invested in *all* the major hotels, getting a great return on their investment and many, many favors. With the Teamsters' bucks in place, Hoffa also ensured that Vegas would be a heavily unionized city. Parking valets belong to the Teamsters Union. Room service waiters and bellhops are union culinary workers. The musicians have their own strong union, theatrical stagehands belong to IATSE (International Alliance of Theatrical Stage Employees), and electrical employees carry IBEW (International Brotherhood of Electrical Workers) cards.

The Teamsters' loans to the casinos were administered by the Valley National Bank. E. Parry Thomas, president of the bank, once explained to a reporter why he worked with the union. "I've got to see that this community stays healthy," he said. "I'll take dollars from the devil himself if it's legal, and I don't mean anything disparaging towards the Teamsters by that."

While many casinos loved the Teamsters' investment, the U.S. Government has not been a big fan. Hoffa lost control of the fund—and lost the Teamsters presidency in 1967—after he was imprisoned on charges of helping to divert $2,000,000 from the fund. In 1972, a special consultant to the fund, Allen Dorfman, was indicted on kickback charges, as was assets manager Alvin Baron in 1976. That same year the IRS, citing mismanagement and questionable loan practices, revoked the Teamsters' fund's tax-exempt status, an action retroactive to 1965.

THE RAT PACK

On June 17, 1960, the historic first Strip hotel, El Rancho Vegas, burned to the ground in the middle of the night. Owner Beldon Kattleman, vowing at a morning-after press conference to rebuild a bigger and even better El Rancho, showed reporters a large piece of metal he had pulled out of the rubble: it was a mass of melted coins worth $417,000.

Nor did the fire dampen visitor interest in Vegas. A greater force was at work, one with more P.R. power than the atom blasts and the Bugsy Siegel rub-out combined. It was hip, it was swinging, it was now. It was Frank Sinatra and his Rat Pack.

The crooner, part owner of the Sands, thought it would be a gas to have his buddies up in Vegas filming a movie by day and working the show room together at night. The 1960 movie was called *Ocean's 11*, about a group of guys who heist money from five Vegas casinos. The stars were Frank, Dean, Sammy, Joey (Bishop), and Peter (Lawford).

"The Sands was the place to be at the time," says Sammy Davis, Jr. "It was hip, it was

Teamsters president Jimmy Hoffa during a 1957 trial; his union invested more money in Las Vegas than anyone else

43

The El Rancho, destroyed by fire on June 17, 1960

BOTTOM LEFT:
"Mr. Warmth" himself, Don Rickles

BOTTOM RIGHT:
Sammy and Jerry performing together at the Sands, 1958

happening. Everybody who was anybody in show business was playing there." And *Ocean's 11* demonstrated to the rest of the world just how hip the Vegas show rooms were. What didn't hurt, either, were newspaper photos showing young presidential candidate John Kennedy coming to town to hang out with Sinatra and his buddies during filming. Nor did the reams of columns waxing poetic about the magic of the Pack, who would perform with each other all night long.

"One of the funniest things that ever happened to me at the Sahara was the time Frank and a bunch of his buddies jumped up onstage, picked me up, and threw me into a waiting cab," recalls Don Rickles. "They took me over to the Sands, where they kept me until the end of my show."

"I was always in the show," says Milton Berle. "Whoever was in the audience would come up and be in the show. We'd do some shtick, sing, and tummel. Just a lot of clowning around and tummeling."

The shows were totally ad-libbed, says Davis, who played "the kid" to Sinatra's "swinger" and Martin's "drunk," and they often lasted through all hours of the night, then continued in the lounge, as Davis, Sinatra, and Martin ad-libbed in the audience while catching Shecky Greene's or Don Rickles's act. The gang would stay up after *that* show and continue the party in Sinatra's Presidential Suite at the Sands. After a very short nap, they met at 5:30 A.M. in the Sands's steam room, then began filming at 6:30.

THE GAMING CONTROL BOARD

The improvised movable feast of the Rat Pack embodied the "anything goes" ethos of vintage Vegas. Back in the early 1940s, before there was such a thing as the Nevada Gaming Commission, that attitude was present at every level and, paramountly, the administrative. The Last Frontier's William J. Moore once told an interviewer that in the early years, eight powerful Reno ranchers, miners, and businessmen—none of whom owned a gambling house—controlled gambling. Moore alleged that they just wanted to widen the state's tax base in order to protect their property for additional taxation. He further suggested that the group controlled how much would

"Laid out from the sky, Las Vegas looks like a vacuum cleaner."

—Don Rickles

The Rat Pack, symbol of Vegas at its most hip, early 1960s; LEFT TO RIGHT: Peter Lawford, Frank Sinatra, Dean Martin, Sammy Davis, Jr., and Joey Bishop

Sam Giancana: enrolled in the Gaming Commission's "Black Book"

be paid to get a gambling license via under-the-counter deals with local law enforcement. "It was going on blatantly," said Moore. "If you went in with enough money, you got a temporary permit." Gambling licenses went to the highest bidder.

Moore, already in place in Las Vegas with the Frontier, was worried about his gaming future. In the 1950s he took on the role of the Vegas gaming lobbyist in Carson City, the state capital, to look out for his interests. "My motive was to stop what was becoming quite obvious to me—too many questionable people working in the business and too many hoodlum factions," he said. "And if it was not controlled, it would wind up a regular shooting war . . . to the point it [legalized gambling] would be voted out by the people."

In 1945 the Nevada State Tax Commission took over the licensing of casinos from the sheriff's office. It was the state's first move to squeeze a little more out of their cash cow. The commission first proposed a straight 10 percent across-the-board tax on revenues. Casino owners said that slice would be way too big, that it would wipe them out. The parties compromised on a tax of 5.75 percent of monthly gross gambling wins over $134,000.

Even with local law enforcement out of the picture and the state in charge, men who were considered criminals in other states were getting licensed to run casinos in Nevada. "You have to look at someone like that through a different pair of glasses," former Nevada Gaming Control Board chief Robbins Cahill told a reporter in the 1950s. "You don't often find a bishop of the church, or a member of the social register who wants to go into gambling. An illegal gambler elsewhere could be a legal gambler here." Applicants were given licenses as a realistic and practical method of ensuring the success of legalized gambling. In Nevada, a licensee could stay out of the slammer if he obeyed the rules and behaved like a citizen. Indeed, the state found the operators' experience a valuable asset. Cahill once said that he preferred dealing with the "so-called mobster" rather than the "businessman" who had been successful and well thought of in other lines of work.

> Whenever you went to the mobster with a problem, you could sit down and talk with him, and he would say, "What do you want us to do about it?" But you hit one of these other people, the legitimate businessman, and all you got was an argument.

Cahill ran the Gaming Control Board division of the Nevada State Tax Commission with just one other person; they investigated and monitored all the gambling in Nevada. They were not always entirely cavalier about licensing known criminals. For example, after the commission learned that a new hotel, the Tropicana, had been financed in part by loans New Orleans gambler "Dandy" Phil Kastel had obtained from New York mobster Frank Costello, it ordered the notes paid up in full immediately—or else. Cahill and the commission had learned about Kastel's secret deal when Costello was shot in New York City. Detectives examining Costello's suit jacket found $800 in cash and a sheet of paper on which was inscribed in neat accountant's handwriting that week's house win at the Trop.

Americans started getting wise to just how involved the mob was in running Las Vegas. In 1959, *Reader's Digest* told of how the Flamingo, New Frontier, Desert Inn, Sands, Sahara, Riviera, Dunes, Stardust, Tropicana, and Royal Nevada had all been funded by "the boys" of Minneapolis, Cleveland, Detroit, Miami, New York, and New Jersey. The magazine explained that it was easy for the boys to move in, since gaming had not been regulated before 1955, when the Tax Commission began licensing and screening applicants. While the commission certainly did a better job than had been done before, it was hardly adequate. In the wake of the *Reader's Digest* article and others that followed, a separate Nevada Gaming Commission was formed in 1959. New regulations were established governing accounting, financial reporting, internal controls, cash counting procedures, and computation of gross gaming revenues.

The new Gaming Commission chief, ex-FBI man Ray Abbaticchio, started warning hotels that things were about to change, and ordered them to keep hoodlums off the premises. In 1960 he published a "black book" with the names, aliases, and mugs of eleven mobsters declared personae non gratae in Nevada casinos. A casino's license would be revoked if any of the men were found on the licensee's property.

In the book was Sam Giancana of Chicago, who was found visiting with Frank Sinatra at his Cal-Neva Lodge in Stateline (near Lake Tahoe). After being called on the carpet by state officials, who threatened revocation, Sinatra chose to sell the lodge and his interest in the Sands. Other characters in the book were found in Vegas casinos and booted out. Not by management, but by the state officials who were on hand to show them the door. Local officials were upset, because the raids on the casinos were bad publicity for Las Vegas, and the black book "victims" complained that their rights were being violated. Nevertheless, Vegas was on the way to cleaning up its act.

HOWARD HUGHES

In the years since the assassination of John F. Kennedy, there have been many theories about a Communist versus a Mafia conspiracy against the president's life. The mob theory is that Chicago boss Sam Giancana helped deliver Chicago votes to get the president elected, mistakenly thinking the new president would lay off "the boys." Instead, JFK's brother Bobby, appointed attorney general, sought to sever the mob's ties to gambling. Whether or not the Kennedy assassination was a mob hit, there is no disputing that the Kennedy brothers applied hard federal pressure on Nevada. The attorney general, who was investigating Jimmy Hoffa and his Teamsters Pension Fund investments, began leaking stories to the media that untold profits from Nevada casinos were being skimmed by the mob. Confident that the eastern underworld had taken over Las Vegas gambling, RFK decided that the situation had national impact because the skimmed casino money was used to finance national mob organizations.

Nevada governor Grant Sawyer, while sensitive to federal concerns, worried about the negative public relations that would result from continued harrassment of Vegas casino owners. Kennedy wanted to stage a well-publicized raid in all the casinos; Sawyer fought him. RFK ordered the FBI to begin surveillance of the casinos, and concealed listening devices were installed in the homes and offices of Nevada residents. Sawyer was not amused. He called the attorney general several nasty names in the press. The feud cost Sawyer his bid for an unprecedented third term as Nevada governor. Paul Laxalt, who promised to cooperate with the federal government, easily beat him in the November 1966 elections.

Clearly, the Nevada electorate wanted to live in a clean state, and Laxalt's position was politically and morally sound. However, the fact remained that gambling was vital to Nevada's prosperity and yet casinos were repugnant to conventional investors. Whatever else they had done, the mob had provided needed operating capital. Barely three weeks after the elections, the answer to this dilemma arrived on a midnight train.

A gray-haired, eccentric old man—with millions in the bank—had decided to come to Las Vegas. An ambulance (present for security, not health reasons) brought him from the railroad station to the Desert Inn. He took over the entire ninth floor, which he never left for four years.

At the time of his arrival, Howard Hughes was *Fortune* magazine's richest man in America, with a bankroll of some $750,000,000 in cash, $546,000,000 of it in proceeds from his sale of TWA. He was also the sole owner of Hughes Tool Company, which manufactured a patented device needed to drill oil wells. Hughes's coming to Las Vegas was steeped in mystery. No one saw him enter; no one saw him leave. Since he hated sunlight, the windows in his suite were blacked out the day he arrived. His top Nevada deputy, former FBI agent Robert Maheu, never had any visual contact with his employer—just telephone talk and correspondence. The only people who ever saw him were his five Mormon nurses, to whom, however, he never spoke, because he was nearly deaf and refused to wear a hearing aid.

Hughes quickly wore out his welcome at the D.I. He and his Mormon aides were not gamblers, and the ninth-floor suites were for players. The D.I.'s Moe Dalitz tried to evict the tycoon after two months. Hughes responded by having Maheu negotiate to buy the building.

E. Parry Thomas, of the Valley National Bank, appraised the building for Hughes and recommended a purchase. Maheu offered $13,200,000 barely a week after the *Chicago Sun-Times* had printed an explosive series about mob profit skimming in Las Vegas—articles written with the assistance of Kennedy's Justice Department. At this moment especially, Hughes was good for Vegas's image. His purchase of the Desert Inn—and the casinos he later added to

Howard Hughes: the Vegas community welcomed his cash and credibility

HOWARD
HUGHES
presents

JANE
RUSSELL

VICTOR
MATURE

THE LAS VEGAS STORY

co-starring VINCENT PRICE with HOAGY CARMICHAEL R K O RADIO

Produced by ROBERT SPARKS · Directed by ROBERT STEVENSON

Screenplay by EARL FELTON and HARRY ESSEX

Lobby card for Howard Hughes's 1952 movie about Las Vegas, featuring his protégé, Jane Russell

his portfolio—was a "public relations breakthrough for Nevada," said the influential *Nevada Report* newsletter, "that could not have been delivered by Madison Avenue for $50,000,000. By getting into the gambling business he convinced millions that gambling can't be dirty or Hughes . . . wouldn't be getting into it."

The town loved him; they just couldn't see him. He refused to leave his room, refused to meet with people. He obtained his gaming license without having to appear before the Gaming Commission, a formality everybody else went through. In exchange for their consideration, he offered to finance the university medical school to the tune of $200,000—$300,000 a year (a pledge never kept).

Hughes formed a new company, Summa, and the buying spree was on. Next purchase was the Sands, for $13.6 million. *Las Vegas Sun* publisher/editor Hank Greenspun sold his KLAS-TV to Hughes for $3,000,000. Hughes proceeded to add the Silver Slipper, Castaways, Frontier, and the Landmark (an unfinished eyesore at the time) to his collection, along with the local Alamo Airways airport and a 200-acre ranch. He became Nevada's largest employer, with 8,000 on the payroll. At their peak, his seven casinos accounted for 16 percent of the state's gross gambling revenues, or $84,000,000 a year. "Welcome to Las Vegas, Howard Hughes's Monopoly set," said Johnny Carson at the Sahara one night. "You ever get the feeling he's going to buy the whole place and shut it down?"

"You're wondering why I don't have a drink in my hand?" Frank Sinatra asked a Sands audience one night. "Howard Hughes bought it."

48

Hughes, who had a much different outlook than the Bugsy Siegels and Tony Corneros who had preceded him, banned hookers, topless showgirls, and dirty jokes from his hotels. What he had in common with "the boys" was a fear of being ripped off. His team of ex-FBI men began James Bondian surveillance of the casinos, watching over everybody with remote cameras, putting on stricter controls in all departments, and scrupulously counting all the beans in the house.

"Hughes destroyed Vegas," says comedian Jack Carter.

It was the final nail in the coffin. First it was removing the Mafia, which removed all the complimentaries. It had been that show people were treated like kings. You could never pick up a tab anywhere you went. Howard Hughes comes in and computerizes everything. He brought in those gray-suited guys with the short haircuts and the ties and ran it like a department store.

Hughes's dream, as he wrote in a memo to Maheu, was to

make Las Vegas as trustworthy and respectable as the New York Stock Exchange—so that Nevada gambling will have the kind of reputation that Lloyds of London has. We can make a really super environmental city of the future here—no smog, no contamination, efficient local government, where the taxpayers pay as little as possible, and get something for their money. . . . I like to think of Las Vegas in terms of a well-dressed man in a dinner jacket, and a beautifully jeweled and furred female getting out of an expensive car. I think that's what the public expects here—to rub shoulders with VIPs and stars etc. possibly dressed in sports clothes. But if so, at least good sports clothes.

The local media and politicians wanted nothing more than to *see* Hughes—in *any* style of clothing. They urged him again and again to meet with them, but a pathological fear of germs prevented such a meeting. He finally compromised, agreeing to a phone conversation with Governor Laxalt. "Hughes has added a degree of credibility to the state that it would have taken years of advertising to secure," Laxalt told reporters afterwards. "Let's face it—Nevada has an image problem—the typical feeling is that sin is rampant here. Anything this man does,

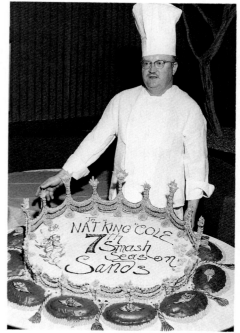

A Sands chef of "chuck," at a fête for Nat "King" Cole

BOTTOM LEFT:
Johnny Carson in Vegas

BOTTOM RIGHT:
Jack Carter: archetypal Vegas comic

"I'm standing next to a slot machine and a woman yanked my arm; my mouth paid off."

—Jack Carter

from the gaming industry all the way down the line, will be good for Nevada." Because of Hughes, the state changed its regulations governing who could apply for a gaming license. Corporations hadn't been allowed in before, because there was no way of knowing exactly who all the investors were. But after Hughes paved the way, Nevada saw investments by Del Webb and by Hilton, Ramada, and other large, publicly traded corporations.

But investing in Nevada and trying to create a utopian community in Las Vegas lost its charm for Hughes when the U.S. Justice Department—and local Vegas officials—started worrying about the potential monopoly Hughes was setting up for himself in town. Attorney General Ramsey Clark opposed his planned purchase of the Stardust. And that opposition was enough for the tycoon to call it a day. He suddenly left town, nearly four years to the day after he arrived in 1970. The old, one-hundred-pound man with a scraggly beard was carried down all nine flights of fire escape stairs and put into an ambulance, which took him to a private plane. Hughes stayed for two years in the Bahamas, a year in Nicaragua and Vancouver, two years in London, another two years in the Bahamas, and then two months in Acapulco, where he died in 1976.

CAESAR AND HIS PALACE

Julius Caesar invaded Britain in 55 B.C. His assault on Vegas took place in 1966, aided by Jimmy Hoffa and his Teamsters, Andy Williams, some pseudo-Roman goddesses, and a visionary named Jay Sarno, who had made his money with a string of Palo Alto, California, "cabana" motels, and whose partner, Nate Jacobsen, had a bankroll of profits from a Baltimore insurance company. Together, they built the gaudiest, weirdest, most elaborate, and most talked-about resort Vegas had ever seen.

The first new Vegas resort since the 1958 Stardust, Sarno's hotel was originally called the Cabana Palace, then the Desert Palace. Finally, it became Caesars Palace, with an emblem of a chesty female dipping grapes into the waiting mouth of a recumbent Roman, fitted out in toga, laurel wreath, and phallic dagger. Sarno thought of everything, from the Roman decor and name to togalike waitress costumes, the hotel logo, the parchmentlike desk stationery, matchbooks and business cards with simulated burned edges (while Nero fiddled . . .). He had long discussions about the apostrophe in "Caesar's"—which he banished because the possessive "would mean it was the place of only one Caesar. We wanted to create the feeling that everybody in the hotel was a Caesar." "Caesars" it became.

Jay Sarno, creator of Caesars Palace and Circus Circus, with Xavier Cugat before the grand opening of Caesars

OPPOSITE:
The eighteen-foot, nine-ton replica of the famous Roman statue of Caesar in the Appian Way at Caesars Palace.

Sarno was the concept and design man. The money was handled by partner Jacobsen. Financing the Palace wasn't easy. "Conservative lending institutions are not interested in Las Vegas because of its image," said Jacobsen at the time. "Most won't even write insurance here."

Hence the call to Jimmy Hoffa.

Of the $25,000,000 spent on building Caesars, $10,600,000 came from the Teamsters. Jacobsen, who had already brokered insurance and profit-sharing plans for several Vegas hotels, spent $1,000,000 on a gala three-day-long opening party, each guest welcomed by the official greeter, a blond 40—20—37 Cleopatra.

Cleo wasn't the only pretty girl at the Palace. There were also the goddesses, long-legged, Greco-Roman-pony-tail-wigged cocktail waitresses, who were instructed to walk up to gamblers and say, "Welcome to Caesars Palace, I am your slave," and then respond to drink orders with "Yes, master." They wore wigs, false eyelashes, and the skimpiest of costumes. They had to learn how to handle a toga drape so that it didn't dip into a martini, and how to bend over in a thigh-length costume without revealing too much behind.

"I had traveled to San Francisco by way of Las Vegas from Texas, and I had noticed that when the plane left Vegas it was almost empty," said Sarno, who died in 1984. "That prompted me to investigate building a hotel here."

But he was quite disappointed after getting a look at the grand hotels he had heard so much about. "The Flamingo was sick—like an old storage room," he said.

The D.I. was a stable. There I was, busting my hump building these slick, gorgeous hotels to make a living, and these bad hotels were making huge sums. I decided I was building in the wrong towns. . . . Las Vegas in the early '60s had done the Wild Western motif to death. What it needed was a little true opulence . . . it was time to do something not too western, but more refined. A Roman-Grecian motif was something new.

Besides the Roman concept, Sarno introduced another design element: oval shapes everywhere.

Over the years that I have been creating hotels, I've discovered that the oval is a magic shape . . . conducive to relaxation. If you examine the Caesars casino, you will find that it is oval-shaped. I even incorporated the oval design into the dice tables, which affects the dice angle geometry. Because the casino is shaped in an oval, people tend to relax and play longer.

The guest list at the opening night party—which featured entertainment by Andy Williams and a full stage show called *Rome Swings*—included Hoffa, David Jannsen of TV's "The Fugitive," and Adam West of "Batman."

"All these movie stars in the lobby couldn't get rooms because the hotel wasn't finished," recalls Williams.

People came into the show room at six for cocktails, but we were so late the show didn't go on until eleven. I remember coming out to this drunken audience, really wacko, and trying to get their attention. I quickly went into "Danny Boy," which is going to get the Irish anyway. I quieted them down by singing it so softly that people in the audience started going *shhhh*.

He also sang the hits "Moon River," "The Shadow of Your Smile," and "What Now, My Love?" as a stage full of goddesses gyrated to the beat.

And what did the first star of the Circus Maximus Room think of the new temple in the desert?

"I thought it was gaudy and awful," says Williams,

OPPOSITE:
Andy Williams opens the Circus Maximus at Caesars Palace.

OVERLEAF:
Inside and outside the one and only Caesars Palace

but I've since come to love it, because everything has gotten worse, and more gaudy and awful. You don't build a hotel in Las Vegas to look like everyone else's home. You need the garish colors, the round beds, the giant bathtubs, because a lot of people come here who have linoleum on their floor, and they want something different. I like very understated things, but if you come to Las Vegas . . . you want that glitzy glamour and sparkle.

CIRCUS CIRCUS

After creating the house of male hedonistic fantasies at the Palace, Sarno went in the totally opposite direction with his next creation in 1968. Circus Circus was a casino without a hotel—just wild animals, balloons, acrobats and high-wire acts, and clowns: the circus, Vegas-style.

"We couldn't believe it," says Sammy Davis, Jr. "Frank called me and said, 'Get this, Smokey—there's a Ferris wheel on the Strip.' We couldn't get over it."

Jay Sarno celebrating the opening of Circus Circus

Low-roller heaven at Circus Circus

Neither could Howard Hughes.

"The aspect of this circus that has me disturbed is the popcorn, peanuts, kids side of it," Hughes wrote in a memo to aide Bob Maheu.

In other words, the poor, dirty, shoddy side of circus life. The dirty floor, sawdust and elephants. It is the above aspects of a circus that I feel are well out of place on the Las Vegas strip. After all, the Strip is supposed to be synonymous with a good looking female all dressed up in a very expensive diamond-studded evening gown and driving up to a multi-million-dollar hotel in a Rolls Royce. Now, you tell me, what in that picture is compatible with a circus and its normal environment, excluding its normal atmosphere and its normal smell.

Indeed, business was rocky at first. On opening day, a large woman climbed onto the circular slide that descended to the bar. She fell, landing atop the bar and smashing several glasses. Another large woman had problems with the firepole that went from the midway on the second floor to the casino on the first floor. She fell and broke both legs.

The slide and firepole are no longer at Circus Circus.

Then there was Sarno's policy of charging admission to tourists to come into the place. "It was one of the craziest ideas anybody ever had," says Mike Hartzell, longtime ringmaster and entertainment director of Circus Circus. "You had to pay at the front door, unless you were a local. If you showed your ID, they let you in for free. But most of our patrons were people coming from other areas, so they would pay to get in, and then pay to gamble, which didn't make any sense. And then pay to see the show."

Sarno—who, unbelievably, envisioned Circus Circus as a high-roller establishment—sold out, broke, in 1974 to William G. Bennett, a businessman who had spent nineteen years managing furniture stores in Arizona before gaming czar Del Webb (Sahara, Mint) hired him to run his gaming properties.

Bennett shucked the elephants, baccarat table, and "comps" (freebies for high rollers) and turned Circus Circus into low-roller heaven. Since Bennett took over, patrons no longer pay to get in, the circus acts are free, a large hotel offers rooms for around thirty dollars and a buffet breakfast for two dollars.

THE INTERNATIONAL

Sarno's next project was going to be the "Grandissimo," a six-thousand-room palace that would, naturally, be the largest resort in the world. It never happened. At "only" 1,519 rooms, Kirk Kerkorian's International Hotel, which opened its doors in 1969, became the largest in America. And with twenty-six floors, each decorated according to a different international theme (Italian, German, Mexican, Japanese, and so on), the International was also the tallest building in Vegas. It had the biggest swimming pool, grandest show room, most restaurants, and largest parking lot in the country—if not the world—or, at least, that's what the hotel said.

Among the biggest problems the day before the debut was the 350,000-gallon pool, which leaked down to the 30,000-square-foot casino, sogging up the 32 blackjack and 12 craps tables and 850 slot machines. Rooms, tables, and restaurants weren't ready on opening day. Cracked Barbra Streisand, paid $250,000 a week to be the International's first headliner on opening night: "Geez, it's just terrific being here at the almost-completed International." (Streisand was followed at the International by Elvis Presley, Don Ho, and Nancy Sinatra.)

Son of an Armenian fruit peddler, Kirk Kerkorian grew up in Fresno, California, moved to Los Angeles, bought and sold used cars, fought as a boxer, and became an aviator. He founded the Los Angeles Air Service in 1947, which served the Del Mar–New York route. He sold the company (renamed Trans International Airlines) to Studebaker in 1962. Then he bought it back for a while and finally re-sold it to Trans America Corporation.

In Las Vegas he bought for $960,000 the forty acres that Caesars stood on and within two years turned around and sold the land to Caesars for $5,000,000. At this point, Kerkorian decided to build the largest resort hotel in the world. He put the $5,000,000 down on sixty-five acres of land on Paradise Road (home of the International) and paid an additional $17,000,000 for the Flamingo, which at the time was floundering in corruption and bankruptcy. Why the Flamingo? Kerkorian purchased it as a training facility for the 2,500 employees who would be working at the new International. When the Flamingo turned around and made bundles of money, Kerkorian kept it as a hotel in its own right.

Kerkorian was quiet and reserved, but he did show up in public and did allow his picture to be taken—a refreshing change from the reclusive Hughes, who worried about the competition he was getting from Kerkorian. At one point, the tycoon instructed aide Robert Maheu to tell Kerkorian that he had information that the Atomic Energy Commission was planning to step up their nuclear tests, and that no tall buildings could survive the blasts. But Kerkorian didn't bite. Hughes responded by buying the Landmark across the street, the strange building Hughes felt could be a Vegas monument, like the Eiffel Tower in Paris. It opened two days before the International.

Casino and Hollywood mogul Kirk Kerkorian in front of his International Hotel, then under construction, later to be known as the Las Vegas Hilton, America's largest hotel

All of his ventures, Kerkorian told *Fortune* in 1969, were tied together by a common thread: exploitation of leisure. And Vegas, he said, was the capital of leisure; where else were you going to find so many pleasure palaces in one city? "Wages are getting higher and hours are getting shorter. People have got to have a place to spend their money." Kerkorian bought the MGM studios in 1970 and sold the International and Flamingo the same year to the Hilton Corporation. The deal set an important precedent in that Hilton became the first major hotel chain to invest in Vegas, paving the way for companies like Ramada, Holiday Inn, and Pratt Hotel Corporation.

"Do you realize that Las Vegas is one of the major hotel cities of the world?" asked Barron Hilton after announcing his new acquisition.

> Do you realize that over 15 million people stayed there last year? That's three-fourths of all the people who visited Florida. It's the entertainment capital of the world and it can be made the convention capital of the world.

By the end of 1970, Las Vegas casino interests had already contributed $4,400,000 to Hilton's bottom line; in 1971 $6,000,000 and $8,500,000 in 1972—50 percent of the company's earnings. Hilton said he was getting in cheap—and said it would prove doubly profitable if he could run the International as efficiently as his other hotels. He was right. Today, more than 70 percent of Hilton's profits come from Nevada.

ALLEN GLICK AND HIS ARGENT CORPORATION

In 1975, *Business Week* wrote a fawning profile of the new Vegas gaming czar Allen Glick, who at the time was the second most powerful force in town, owner/operator of the Stardust, Fremont, Hacienda, and Marina hotels.

"He's the great American success story," Peter Echeverria, then chairman of the Nevada Gaming Commission, told the magazine. "The people who hold our licenses in Nevada are professional businessmen. The old cigar-chewing gambler carrying a holster is gone."

Glick told the magazine that tales of mob interference in Vegas were "fiction." "Las Vegas is an intriguing place, and people like to fantasize about it. Gaming is actually a highly regulated industry."

Before joining the gaming world, Glick was a young San Diego-area lawyer, making eight hundred dollars a month selling apartments and condos. He then hooked up with the Saratoga Development Company, where he continued in real estate. Saratoga found his services so valuable that the company sold him a 45-percent share of the $4,500,000 firm for $2,500. Glick then formed another company, Argent (French for "money") Corporation, moved to Vegas, and, with financing from Saratoga and the Teamsters Pension Fund, bought and operated the four major casino/hotels. (These were no small loans from the union. The Teamsters lent nearly $150,000,000 for the four properties.)

Glick's right-hand man in Argent was Frank "Lefty" Rosenthal, who served as entertainment director. A TV talk-show host and newspaper columnist, Rosenthal was (the FBI alleged) a frontman for the Chicago mob. In 1988 the Nevada Gaming Commission nominated him for inclusion in its notorious "black book" of those banned from licensed gaming properties.

Glick's Las Vegas reign was brief. He was forced out of the casino business by Nevada gaming authorities in 1979 when they discovered a $7-million-dollar slot-skimming scam at the Stardust. Glick later admitted to the FBI that he had indeed been a front for the mob—albeit an unwilling front; they had made him an offer he couldn't refuse; Glick feared for his life.

THE MGM GRAND

With the MGM Studios as the latest addition to his portfolio, Kirk Kerkorian returned to Las Vegas and the casino biz. To finance his new production—the MGM Grand Hotel—he sold off most of his MGM assets and brought the film production schedule down to around five movies a year, saying films weren't very profitable anymore. But the movie studio did provide a terrific new theme for a new Vegas hotel—movie nostalgia. The Grand was named after the 1932 MGM classic *Grand Hotel*, and its rooms were named after MGM stars like Spencer Tracy, Clark Gable, Wallace Beery, and Judy Garland; its grand suites bore movie titles, like *Ben-Hur* and *Mrs. Miniver*. The $120,000,000, 2,100-room hotel with 4,500 employees was for a time the largest in America, eclipsing the International. (When the Las Vegas Hilton added a second wing in 1973, the MGM became the second largest. The Hilton currently boasts 3,174 rooms.)

The Grand bought 125,000 square yards of carpet, worth $1,250,000—enough carpet, hotel publicists said, to stretch all the way from Las Vegas to Garden Grove, California. Some

Dean Martin opening the MGM Grand

Kerkorian's MGM Grand

5,000 trees were cut down in North Carolina to produce 32,000 separate pieces of furniture, which incorporated 42,000 items of hardware. In addition, 1,895 miles of electric wiring, 200,000 light bulbs, and 50,000 lighting fixtures were installed.

Opening night, with Dean Martin providing the entertainment, was no ordinary hotel debut; it was a star-studded movie premiere. Cary Grant, Fred MacMurray, Barbara Eden, and Jane Powell clapped the clapper that said "MGM Grand, Scene One, Take One," and the party began.

The Nixon-Ford recession did little to discourage guests from dropping big money at the Grand's gaming tables and slots. In 1974, after its first full year of operation, the MGM Grand returned the highest net profits and revenues in the fifty-eight-year history of MGM Corporation. Of the company's $28,600,000 in profits that year, the Grand was responsible for $22,000,000.

For eight years, the hotel had a "boffo" run. But then came November 21, 1980, and "The Towering Inferno."

The night before the fire, the MGM Grand was 99 percent full, with guests in town from all over the world. Many of them were in the MGM's Celebrity Room, watching entertainer Mac Davis. Onstage, the writer of Elvis Presley's hit "In the Ghetto" sang a tribute to Elvis, which he had just written, called "Something's Burnin'."

By morning, something was.

Around seven A.M. the MGM's football field-size casino was nearly empty and the restaurants

The Big Fire

were beginning to fill up with guests for breakfast. The first clue that this would be a very long, sad day came when a waitress saw flames coming out of the keno board in the "Deli." Sixty seconds later, it was apparent that the entire hotel was ablaze. By the end of the day seven hundred people would be injured and eighty-four killed.

It was the worst disaster ever to hit Las Vegas.

Producer Donn Arden (*Lido de Paris, Hallelujah Hollywood*) is known in Las Vegas as the "Master of Disaster." His shows have featured the sinking of the *Titanic*, the eruption of a volcano, the explosion of the *Hindenburg*, and the bursting of a big dam. But Arden's greatest disaster took place in his tenth-floor suite on November 21, 1981.

Hallelujah Hollywood had just closed, and Arden, who lives in Palm Springs and Mission Viejo, California, was putting together a new show, *Donn Arden's Jubilee!*, scheduled to open at the Grand in three weeks. He shared his suite with frequent collaborator Madame Bluebell.

"Around seven A.M. all hell started breaking loose," recalls Arden.

They were knocking on doors and saying, "Wake up! Fire! Wake up! Fire!" I looked out in the hall, and all I saw was smoke. I went into Bluebell's room and said "Bluebell,

62

you've got to get up! There's a fire!" So she managed to put on her mink coat over her nightie, and I just put on a long bathrobe I had in my room, and we headed towards the elevators.

We'd go a hundred feet, and we'd run into people, and they'd say, "Don't go that way, you won't be able to get out." And so they're all pushing us back from where we came. We went to the stairwells, and the stairwell doors were locked. We didn't know what to do, so we went back into our suite, and following us were ten people, too. They were locked out because they didn't have their keys. We look out over the balcony, and we see flames here and there.

Flamingo Boulevard [the MGM is on Flamingo and Las Vegas boulevards] is full of fire wagons, and they're yelling instructions in Spanish and English and what have you over these speakers, and there's constant rapping on my door, more and more people are coming in. Our living room is just jammed.

Well, believe it or not, what's awful about the thing is that some of the people I allowed into the suite, you know, I discovered them going through my drawers and stealing money. Isn't it awful?

Finally, they told us that the ladders would only go as far as the ninth floor. But we were on the side where the ramp was, and the ramp made it possible for the ladders to come up to ten. All the people started climbing onto the ladder and going down.

Then there was this fat lady who had just lost her daughter. There was no way that woman could ever go from that balcony to that small ladder, never, and she was out of her mind already. She was saying, "Why don't we all just sit down and order room service?" She had lost her mind.

There's a knock on the door, and it's a fireman, all smudged in black, who had figured a way for us to go down the stairwell. I had a big wet bar, and I had been using soda, tonic water, ice cubes, anything, to put moisture on people's faces. By the time he got there all I had left was vodka. So we wrapped our faces in vodka and started going down the stairwell.

They had little Christmas-tree lights down the stairwell every twenty feet, but it was virtually pitch black. We got to the bottom, then stepped in water up to our knees. It was terrible; my beautiful, new, five-thousand-dollar costumes were floating in the water.

I walked to the corner of Flamingo and the Strip [Las Vegas Boulevard], and there was the roof of my theater with all of the smoke coming out of it. All of my costumes, all of my scenery—gone.

Yet, nine months later, with a new set of costumes, scenery, and many new cast members (after the fire, most of the dancers had to find more immediate work in other shows), *Donn Arden's Jubilee!* opened—and the MGM Grand reopened.

The cause of the fire was electrical equipment that hadn't been grounded properly and caused the wiring to overheat and burn. The hotel—like most others in Las Vegas—had no in-room fire sprinklers; at the time, the law didn't require them. MGM Grand chairman Fred Benninger announced shortly after the fire that the hotel would install

every safety feature available within the state of the art. The safety features will be the latest, and the state of the art will take precedence over the demands of the laws.

Other hotels announced that they would also upgrade their fire-protection systems. When the MGM reopened on July 29, 1981, Nevada law required sprinkler systems in all hotels, office buildings, and apartment buildings taller than fifty-five feet; sprinklers were mandatory in show rooms and other public gathering places of more than five thousand square feet. In January 1983, MGM agreed to pay $75,000,000 out of a total $140,000,000 settlement to 1,357 survivors and relatives of fire victims.

63

Boardwalk and beach, Atlantic City

ATLANTIC CITY AND THE GREAT RECESSION OF 1981

The fire was not the only catastrophe Vegas faced. In 1978, roughly one year after New Jersey voters passed the Casino Control Act, Resorts International, the first legal non-Nevada casino in the continental United States, opened its doors.

People stood in line several blocks down the Boardwalk to get in; once inside, they refused to leave the tables. Business was so brisk that customers had to wait in line just for a space at a twenty-one table. In its first twelve months, Resorts racked up very impressive opening figures: gross gaming revenue of $228,000,000—28 percent more than the seven casinos of South Lake Tahoe combined, for the comparable period.

The reasons for the millions were simple. Atlantic City wasn't in the middle of a desert. Some sixty million people live within three hundred miles of the seaside resort community; Philadelphia is just sixty miles away; New York and Newark one hundred miles. The Atlantic City casinos appeal to people who buy lottery tickets in hopes of hitting it big as well as to Wall Street types willing to drop thousands a day on the tables without feeling hurt at all.

New Jersey voters said yes to gambling in Atlantic City in an effort to restore the historic resort city to its former glory. The home of the Miss America pageant had fallen on grave times, with crime and slums the main topics of conversation. Gambling interests in Las Vegas were scared to death about their new competition. They figured it could be the beginning of the end. But instead of sitting at home and worrying, many decided to join the fray.

"Coming to Atlantic City took about as much perspicacity as biting into this cheesesteak [I'm eating]," the Golden Nugget's Steve Wynn told *Fortune* in 1980.

> I took one look at Resorts. It was June 16 [1978], a couple of weeks after it had opened, and I'll never forget standing on the steps [leading into the casino]. I saw more people betting more money than I'd ever seen in my life. It made Caesars Palace . . . on New Year's Eve look like it was closed for lunch.

Wynn had an easier time establishing the Atlantic City Golden Nugget than did the Vegas corporation that opened the second Atlantic City casino, Caesars Boardwalk Regency, in 1979. The company was granted a New Jersey gaming license on one condition—that its owners, Cliff and Stuart Perlman, sell their interests in the corporation. New Jersey officials were set against the Perlmans because of a relationship with a Florida lawyer the state said was an "associate" of mobster Meyer Lansky. The brothers sold their shares for $100,000,000.

Ramada (owners of the Tropicana), the Showboat, and Harrah's (owned by Holiday Inn) all had a relatively easy time getting licensed, although Hilton Corporation was rejected after it put little effort into the licensing process. Non-Vegas interests also set up shop in Atlantic City, most notably New York real estate developer Donald Trump, Bally's, and Playboy.

As Atlantic City's fortunes rose, the bubble began to burst in Las Vegas. By 1981, some three thousand new hotel rooms were being built, yet fewer visitors came to visit, discouraged by high airfares and the recession. The devaluation of the peso kept Mexican big spenders away, the 1982 collapse of the Hong Kong stock exchange devastated some prime customers from Asia, skidding oil prices knocked out a lot of Texans and Arabs, and casino owners were left with millions in uncollectable markers. Six casinos folded; the Riviera filed for protection under chapter eleven.

In 1982 fewer people came to Vegas than the year before (11.6 million vs. 11.8 million), while Atlantic City attracted 21 million.

But that's not the end of the story. The crime and slums of Atlantic City are still big problems. The casinos provide their own little fantasylands inside, but it's no fun getting to them. And the pool of visitors, it seems, is finite. Each new casino opening doesn't increase overall business, but instead slices the pie a little thinner. Indeed, once the recession eased, the novelty of Atlantic City began to wear off. Its casinos, after all, were more crowded than those in Vegas, and rooms, food, and parking cost much more. With new attractions like big boxing matches and conventions, and lower airfares from deregulated airlines, Las Vegas made a big comeback. In 1987, some thirty million had come to visit Atlantic City, compared with sixteen for Vegas. But those who came out West spent more. The gross gaming revenue for all the Atlantic City hotel/casinos in 1987 was $2,500,000,000; for Vegas, $2,700,000,000.

Artist's rendering of the revitalized Atlantic City

ATLANTIC CITY

Ask anybody in Vegas and they'll gladly tell you that Atlantic City stinks.

It's a dump, crime-infested; nobody wants to stay there overnight. The four hotels on the corner of Las Vegas and Flamingo boulevards—Bally's, Caesars, the Dunes, and the Flamingo Hilton—have more hotel rooms between them than all the Atlantic City hotels combined. Atlantic City has no race and sports betting, no poker, no topless showgirls.

But what Atlantic City does have is location. The famous statistic: thirty-seven million adult Americans are only a gas-tank away. Because of its proximity to so many large urban centers (New York, Philadelphia, Newark, Washington, and Boston) Atlantic City has about twice the number of visitors each year that Vegas has, yet gamblers there lose about the same amount of dough ($2,500,000,000 in Atlantic City in 1987 compared to $2,700,000,000 in Vegas), and more casinos are losing money in Atlantic City, while in Las Vegas, most are making piles of profits.

What it all comes down to is weather.

"Vegas is year 'round," says Sam Distefano, the entertainment director of the Riviera, who spent many years working in Atlantic City at Playboy's casino.

In Atlantic City, regardless of what they say, come October—March, it's wintertime, my friend, and a Friday—Saturday town. People come to Vegas for three- to four-day vacations. In Atlantic City you drive in and out. Okay, so there are thirty million visitors in Atlantic City versus fifteen million here. The difference is that some of those people are counted three or four times. I know of ladies that would come on bus tours twice a day from New York. In the summer they would pay them $10 worth of quarters to come—and feed them. So these women would get up at seven A.M., drive out on an air-conditioned bus, get a free lunch and a roll of quarters, and be back by noon. Then they'd return at two o'clock. They were making $20 a day, having free meals, and hanging out with their friends in air-conditioned comfort.

In Atlantic City it costs you $8 to park your car. There are no buffets in Atlantic City. For a guy that's retired and wants to move somewhere, he can come here [to Vegas] and have a 49¢ breakfast. Sure, it's not going to be steak and chops, but a lot of people are happy with it. For 49¢ you can get ham and sausage and eggs. It's cheaper to eat out here, and you don't have to worry about sub-zero weather. That's why this town is growing and expanding.

OLD DAYS AND NEW

By the end of the 1980s, the crowds in Vegas were larger than ever, and the city of 700,000 residents had become quite different from the western resort founded by gangsters forty years earlier.

"Vegas in the '50s was made for the big gambler," says Bill Boyd of the Boyd Group, owners of four Vegas hotels, including the Stardust and Fremont.

> The town was not made for the working stiff to come here and play, because he had no money, and there were no rooms for him. We didn't have hotels, we had motels with a hundred fifty to two hundred rooms. The place was made for the guy who wanted some action.
>
> We didn't have million-dollar slots back then. We didn't have conventions. The gambler who came here was a businessman with some hidden money or some cash to spend, and he had to know someone in the gambling business who would give him credit.
>
> Today, the Strip has become Middle America. The Strip and downtown markets are coming towards each other, and they're more competitive. At one time the markets were very different. The Strip was higher-income than downtown was. Personally, I like the fact that when you get out to dinner or a show you dress up, but I think a lot of Middle America is uncomfortable with that. They come to Las Vegas to vacation and feel more comfortable being more casual.

"I wish I could convey to you what it was like to walk out on that stage in the old days," says Sammy Davis, Jr.

In the good old Vegas days, says Sammy Davis, Jr., "You'd go onstage and say good evening, and it was like a New York setting."

The classic Downtown Vegas look of the "Good Old Days"

First, there would be that exodus around four-thirty or five from the pool area, people in their cashmeres or whatever; it was casual. The women went to the hairdressers— the men to the steam room—went back to the room, and, six-thirty to seven, look out! You saw chicks walking out, and you'd do double takes. You had seen them in the earlier part of the day, and you didn't know they looked that good. It was so glamorous. You'd go out onstage and say good evening, and it was like a New York setting.

I realize the Strip should be fun for everyone, but if you want to come see Frank Sinatra, or Sammy and Jerry, hey, you've got to put on a jacket—open collar if you must. You want to gamble in the daytime, do what you must; but at night, fellas, we need the jacket on. But they won't say it; they're so afraid of losing that dollar.

"I have to be very careful," says Wayne Newton.

One reason is my intellect tells me that the good old days are ahead of us, but my heart tells me that Sammy and I will never see the town as we knew it again. I think that's called progress.

The town has switched from being a place that goes from midnight to six A.M., to being totally and completely a convention city, which is the reason that a lot of hotels are having a really tough time doing business in the second shows, because those people have to get up in the mornings for their meetings. There are only four show rooms left that book stars, and yet there aren't enough stars to fill those show rooms.

"There was an intimacy about Las Vegas in those days," says Davis. "It was almost like family: everybody knew everybody. Now you could take all the employees of the biggest hotels and put them all together in a room. They'd all be wearing brown shoes and white socks. Mentally they're just not Vegas type of people."

68

The late 1980s have seen the greatest building boom in Vegas history. New hotels by the owners of the Golden Nugget, Flamingo Hilton, and Circus Circus began construction, as did additions to the Riviera, Sahara, and Imperial Palace. The new owners of the Sands announced plans to add on, and several other firms said they would build additional pleasure palaces.

Vegas as a convention city—this one's a convocation of pizza product producers

All told, we're talking a minimum addition of 20,000 hotel rooms, bringing the grand total to around 80,000, more rooms than many cities have population.

To say the money men have been bullish is an understatement.

"When you have a market in Vegas that already is worldwide, when you have a market that already has 60,000 rooms, 80 percent occupied fifty-two weeks a year, you can toss two or three thousand rooms in there and, in a down market, just by being the best and the newest, be assured of full occupancy," says the Golden Nugget's Steve Wynn.

Las Vegas is about to explode. It's got its own force. It's so big now, it feeds on itself. We've got tremendous momentum. There's an infrastructure here of conventions and organizations. No matter what we do, there's no way we're going to get the high roller here Sunday through Thursday. He's at his business. So each hotel has high-priced guys beating the bushes, afraid to death that their mid-week occupancy will go down the drain. They're making deals with wholesalers, meeting groups, doing every trick in the book to get people in here Sunday through Thursday. It's had an effect.

Atlantic City never attracts many conventions because there aren't enough hotel rooms in town to support them. But Las Vegas stays in business because of all the mid-week conventions, which fill up the hotel rooms and put dollars in the casinos, restaurants, and other local businesses.

69

Flamingo flamingo and Sahara camel

The Las Vegas Convention and Visitors Authority spent much of the decade publicizing the fact that their city had become the number-two convention town in America, right after Chicago—not a bad feat, considering that Chicago is America's third-largest city and Vegas stands at seventieth.

Meanwhile . . .

• The neon strip of El Rancho's sign still glows every night on the Strip. But this El Rancho bears no relation to the historic first Vegas resort. That one burned to the ground in 1960. To this day, the land it sat on (across the street from the Sahara) remains vacant. The new El Rancho sits between the Sahara and Riviera on the other side of the street, on the site of the old Thunderbird Hotel.

• Soon after the New Frontier became just the Frontier in 1967, Howard Hughes bought it. The home of the hottest show in town from 1981 to 1988—Siegfried and Roy's *Beyond Belief*—the Frontier was sold in 1988 to Margaret Elardi, who turned the hotel's famous show room (where Siegfried and Roy, Wayne Newton, and Sammy Davis, Jr., all performed) into a coffee shop.

• Several mob consortia ran the Flamingo until 1967, when Kirk Kerkorian bought it. (Morris Lansburgh and his Flamingo partners pleaded guilty in 1973 to a $36,000,000 skim operation that took place at the Flamingo from 1960 to 1967.) Kerkorian sold the Flamingo and International to the Hilton Corporation in 1970. The original motellike rooms of the Flamingo still exist, in back, by the pool; most people stay in the two large towers—total, 3,000 rooms—that the Hilton organization added. And there's more coming: another tower is being added, which will bring the room total to over 3,500.

• Kerkorian sold his MGM Grand to the Bally Corporation in 1986. According to the terms of the purchase, Bally had two years to remove MGM's Leo the Lion from all the carpets and pull the movie-star pictures off the walls. No, the new corporate mascot isn't Bally's Ms. Pac-Man.

• Out of Las Vegas for two years, Kerkorian returned in 1988 and bought the Desert Inn and the Sands from Hughes's Summa Corporation for over $150,000,000. Within three months, he sold the Sands to Sheldon Adelson, the entrepreneur behind the mammoth COMDEX (computer dealers) convention.

• After years of bad business culminating in operation under Chapter 11 bankruptcy, the Riviera was bought in 1980 by multimillionaire Meshulam Riklis (Mr. Pia Zadora), who turned the hotel around. The exclusive, Miami-styled resort became the first to have a fast-food restaurant—a Burger King—on its premises. Riklis also added more shows (four), a pizzeria, and a coffee shop named after his daughter (Kady's Brasserie). The Riv at last escaped bankruptcy. With the addition of many new towers, its room count (at this writing) is set to top four thousand.

• By the end of 1989, the six largest hotels in America were projected for Las Vegas. Additions at the Riviera were scheduled to bring its room count to 4,179; then there's the new Excalibur, from Circus Circus, with 4,000 rooms; Steve Wynn's new 3,600-room Mirage; the remodeled Flamingo Hilton at 3,558 rooms; the Las Vegas Hilton at 3,174; and Bally's at 3,100.

PART
TWO

GAMBLING.
GAMBLERS
& GAMES

CHAPTER 4

The Gambling Business

The gambling business, as anyone in Vegas will gladly tell you, has hardly changed at all since the formative years of the early 1900s. The tables are still green, an ace and a king still qualifies as instant blackjack, and the pit boss still stands in the pit watching the game. The casino is still dark, with no clocks or daylight found anywhere, and players still lose more than they win.

But there *is* something different in the casino that separates the old from the new: that big computer in the gaming pit. And it keeps track of everything the bosses used to have to juggle in their brains.

"In the past, you really didn't know what you were making," says former Frontier shift manager Carmen Rizzo. "You thought you knew how much the guy was playing, but you really didn't. Now you can track the customer [with the computer] and see they weren't the customer you once thought they were."

The computer makes the decision on whether or not the gambler should qualify for the highest honor Las Vegas can bestow: RFB—free room, food, and beverage. Everything free. Possibly even airfare.

"It's just like any other business," says Caesars Palace assistant vice president Lee Rice. "If you're selling dolls and one customer buys ten dolls a year, you treat him differently from the customer who buys one thousand a year."

The rule of thumb is that the longer you play at the tables, the more complimentary goodies you are entitled to. Gamble $1,000 in an hour, that's maybe good for a free meal. Drop $5,000 in a couple of hours, you might be eligible for show tickets and some meals. But part with $5,000 an hour for four hours a day—the minimum to be considered a really big player—and chances are you'll get the RFB.

But is it really worth it? More players lose than win, and it certainly would be a lot cheaper just to pay your own way. Of course, then you wouldn't be treated like a king. By spending all that money at the tables and getting the RFB treatment, you're buying Vegas status. "To be able to say, 'I was treated in such and such a fashion at Caesars Palace,'" says Rice, "to be able to go back to the country club at home and say, 'I'm a High Roller at Caesars Palace...'"

It's with the computer that the gambling house figures out whether Mr. Big Player gambled $50,000 over the weekend or not. The pit girl tracks the players as they sit down, entering the exact number of minutes of play, average bet per hand, winnings and losses, and other information. The computer printout at the end of the visit shows the player's name, home address, and phone number, employer, and gaming statistics. At the bottom is a profit and loss statement on the player, deducting restaurant and room charges from the gambling win.

Each casino has different criteria for high-roller status. All it takes is buying $500 worth of chips at the Stardust, and at upper-market places, like Caesars and the Las Vegas Hilton, $25,000 tends to be the starting point. Five thousand dollars will usually buy high-roller treatment at the mid-market casinos. "If you want a full RFB, that's a $75 average with a minimum of four hours playing time per day," says one mid-market casino shift manager. Which means an average $75 bet on blackjack for every hand you play—and that could be eighty hands an hour. "We don't care if you play $50 for awhile, and then $100 for a while, just as long as you maintain a $75 average over your period of stay. If you stay here for three days, we expect twelve hours of playing time."

Former Frontier shift manager Carmen Rizzo in front of his computer, used to track how players are betting

OPPOSITE LEFT:
"Free slot pull!" says the downtown hawker.

OPPOSITE RIGHT:
Gambling at Circus Circus, 1968— distracted neither by clown nor by daring young men on the flying trapeze

OPPOSITE BOTTOM:
Vegas casino at high tide

73

Roulette—not the best bet in Vegas

For the ultimate in RFB, and to really bask in the true Las Vegas fantasy experience, try one of the eight "Classic" suites at the Las Vegas Hilton. The Gold Coast room features an Indiana Jones *"Raiders of the Lost Ark"* exotic theme, while the Hollywood Suite is strictly black-and-white nostalgia. All are on the twenty-ninth floor, with a sweeping view of virtually the entire Strip.

But don't try asking for one of the Classics next time you check in. They are reserved for the Hilton's favorite gambling customers, which means those who gamble $750,000 or more over the weekend—or $1,500 a hand on the various games.

The Caesars High Roller isn't just a big gambler; he is a "noble friend" who gets greeted at the airport—and at parties—by the exotic Caesars "Vestal Virgin." The only requirements are that he "be a customer who has the ability to play and lose $50,000 or more and plays in a manner in which we would reasonably expect that he could lose such sums."

But, seriously, why would anyone be willing to give away $50,000?

"Look at it on this level," says Bill Cosby.

You play two-hand touch, then you have guys who play high school football, then you have guys who play college football. That's another level of thinking. Now from that you move to the pros, which is *another* level of thinking. By the time these guys reach $20,000 a hand, they're into the business. That $20,000 could be *your* life— *you'd* put so much weight on those two cards. But for *them* it's not even one hand. It's three or four hands a person, trying to play catch-up. It's what they call steaming. That's where guys can either collapse or rise to the occasion. And that's what the casinos like to see, but they don't care for it if the guy turns out to be right, because, boom, their spirits go straight down.

"I don't know what those guys could be doing if it wasn't gambling," says local comedian Pete Barbutti.

What are they going to do, find a chick? With that kind of money, they've had most of the chicks they're going to have. Where are they going to go? Cleveland is pretty uninteresting. So what are they going to do with their money, especially guys in oil,

74

where you make $10,000 a day whether you get out of bed or not? You have a Lear jet; you don't need two. You have a big boat; you don't need another. So once you've paid for the plane and the boat and the Lamborghini, what else do you need? Because there's still plenty of money coming in every day. So you gamble. It's the challenge of doing it.

These big-time gamblers come from faraway places, like Saudi Arabia, Korea, Singapore, Japan, as well as from Texas, California, the East, West, and Midwest. Ninety-nine percent of the time they are male; Vegas casinos were created with men in mind.

What helped bring about the emergence of the medium- and low-roller casino was a law that went into effect in 1984. From that year on, anyone who gambled more than $10,000 had to file a form with the casino, which reported it to the IRS. Drug dealers and other people who didn't want the government knowing about their lives stopped coming to Vegas.

Golden Nugget chairman Steve Wynn has said there are only about one thousand bona fide high rollers out of a universe of big gamblers, whom he classifies as follows:
• 15,000–20,000 people who will spend $5,000 a weekend at the tables
• 10,000 $25,000-a-weekend gamblers
• 1,000 $50,000-and-up gamblers

"Those [the 1,000 $50K men] are the guys that we fly in on the jet at our expense and get our finest penthouse suites," says Wynn.

One thousand is actually quite a bit. All you want is five or ten of them to play at a time. They can make a day that can create a $500,000 drop [house win] in one day.

"Asking me to stop gambling is like telling Marilyn Monroe not to show five inches of her cleavage."

—Milton Berle

Stardust casino manager Buddy Spach holding the tools of his trade—his chips

The high-roller business isn't real lucrative, but it's important because the regular people want to be around them. You get an awful lot of free business from guys, who have four to five thousand dollars to bet, who like being around these people.

Caesars, the acknowledged king of the high-roller business, can make as much in one day from one guy losing $500,000 as the king of the low rollers, Circus Circus, can make on that day in their entire casino. On the other hand, when one of the super Caesars players—known as a "whale"—comes to visit and wins, the casino can get hit pretty bad. Caesars is said to have fifty losing days a year.

Gamblers lost nearly $3,000,000,000 at the tables and slots in the Las Vegas area in 1987. The casino that cleaned up more loot than any other was, as usual, Caesars, the most profitable house in town, with a yearly win of around $200,000,000. The numbers vary from year to year, but the five Vegas casinos that show the greatest casino profits are Caesars, the Las Vegas and Flamingo Hiltons, Circus Circus, and Bally's, in that order.

The house bosses are always on the prowl for new big customers, but it's rare that they find them. "The chances of you walking in here and putting down $2,000 cold on a hand of twenty-one are very, very slim, almost impossible," says Buddy Spach, casino manager of the Stardust.

The world of gamblers is very small. We know everybody. Just like everybody in the tennis business knows anybody that's a tennis player, and everybody in the golfing business knows who's who in the golf business, we know the gambling community.

But let's say Joe Gambler decides to come into the Stardust one night, take a seat at the twenty-one table, and start wagering $100 a hand on the game. He'll find that he has quickly made some new friends.

"This guy puts some money down on the table, the floor man is going to cut into him and ask him if he'll have some dinner and ask for his name," says Spach.

We'll run a check on him, ask where he's from, where he's staying, where he plays. By the time he gets through playing, we'll know whether he's a player or not. Plus we'll be seeing by his money on the table whether he knows how to play or not.

A good day in a medium-sized casino is characterized as something between $200,000 and $300,000 in winnings—more loot than most people will see in several years of employment. So it's not too hard to understand why the first thing a casino executive does each morning when he comes to work is check the win/loss statement.

"It's probably silly to do that, but it's just become habit," says Paul Lowden, chairman of the Sahara and Hacienda hotels. "It's like checking the cash register of a retail store. It really doesn't matter, because at the end of the year, you're going to end up with the same 19 to 20 percent win." It's this percentage that always takes care of the house. In other words, luck really doesn't mean anything; the house is always in the driver's seat. The longer a gambler plays, the better the odds are that the house will win back its money. And if the player doesn't give it back today, he'll certainly return it tomorrow.

"The way I look at it, if a customer wins any kind of money at all, we're just loaning it to him for a short period of time," says Rizzo. "Because we're just a bank. They're going to come back."

"You really rob yourself if you stay too long at the tables," says Bill Cosby, who has spent many a night in the baccarat pit. "Sometimes you have to make up your mind if you really want to win or you're just there for the action. Because if you're just there for the action, which is what I was there for, you're going to lose."

The gamblers who have moved to Las Vegas learned a long time ago that the only way to get rich gambling is to own a casino.

"If you play and you play long enough, you must pay," says Jack Binion of the Horseshoe.

"The odds are going to catch up to you. The key is to use gambling as a form of entertainment instead of trying to get rich."

Professional Vegas gamblers won't even spend minutes—let alone hours—at twenty-one, dice, or baccarat. They won't play the table games at all. "Anyone who plays those games is just throwing their money away. You can't possibly win," says local gambler Lem Banker, who has made hundreds of thousands of dollars betting every day in Vegas—on sports games. The only money maker in town besides sports, he says, is a good high-stakes poker game.

Where money *can* be made in the casinos is by cheating. A multi-million-dollar business exists in the underbelly of Vegas, with slot, twenty-one, dice, and baccarat cheats. That's why all the casinos have elaborate "eye-in-the-sky" electronic surveillance systems that monitor every game in the house. The number of TV monitors in the eye-in-the-sky room can be as few as four in a small place like the Bourbon Street Casino or as many as fifty at the Las Vegas Hilton. There are also large banks of VCRs, which tape the proceedings; the recordings are kept for three days as a check against potential complaints from customers, the Gaming Commission, or internal management.

Winning doesn't bother me," says Bill Boyd, chairman of the Boyd Group, owner of the Stardust, Fremont, California, and Sam's Town,

unless I feel I could have been cheated. Cheating is very common. There are professional cheaters out there. I think there is more money lost in slot machine cheaters than anything else. It's an untold amount. We have all types of electronic surveillance methods to prevent cheating, but as fast as you plug up one hole in slots, the cheater will find another one. . . . It's kind of like the retail business, where you've constantly got shoplifting. You have to factor that in, because you're going to have it. You need to keep it at the minimum if you're going to be successful.

At the tables, dealers are always suspect in cheating escapades, because bosses worry they could be in cahoots with players. That's one of the reasons most casinos won't allow dealers to talk to players. Another is that they don't want to offend the losing player. "You get a situation where a guy is hunched over the table, and he's just lost $8,000, he doesn't want to hear a

The eye-in-the-sky room at the Las Vegas Hilton: television cameras monitor all casino activity, and VCRs record it

Sahara owner Paul Lowden in his eye-in-the-sky room

HARD AND SOFT COUNTS

Every morning, from four to seven A.M., a team of men boards a large vehicle, loads it with large silver buckets, and sweeps the casino, emptying the slot machines. The team is accompanied by two security guards and a video camera, which watches their every step.

A locked cabinet under the slot machine is opened, revealing a silver bucket filled with coins. This is pulled out of the cabinet and replaced with an empty bucket from the vehicle.

Some of the buckets collected are not very full—the product of a "loose" slot, which has paid off well that day. Some buckets overflow, coins bursting out of the opened slot cabinet. Such machines have not been very kind to gamblers that day.

Once the buckets have been pulled out of every slot in the house, the team drives into the back room behind the casino cage, where no civilians—and few employees—are ever allowed. It is the count room—site of all the infamous casino mob "skims"

through the years, when owners, disregarding the honor system, deducted a share of the winnings to send home to "the boys" back East.

Actually, there are two count rooms—the "soft count" for folding money and the "hard count" for coin. The hard count begins with employees dumping the coins into giant machines, which automatically process the pile into rolls of coins. The machines are programmed into a computer, so that by the end of the process, the house knows exactly how many coins have been collected in winnings. The "soft count" is a much more tedious, old-fashioned process. It begins with emptying out boxes of bills from the casino floor. These boxes, which are locked underneath the gaming tables, are collected three times a day—after the day, swing, and graveyard shifts. They are then brought back to the soft-count room, across the hall from the hard-count room, where they are locked up, waiting for the

Top left, right, and bottom left: hard counters at work in the early morning collecting coins; bottom right: a Las Vegas Hilton guard watching over the cash.

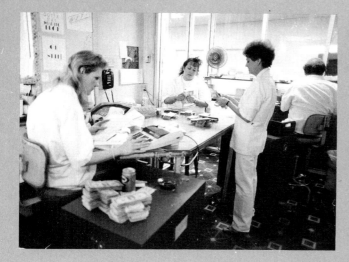

In the cage: a cashier at the Aladdin Hotel

"This isn't money," says a counter in
the soft-count room at the Sahara,
"it's just paper."

counters, who arrive in teams of three or four first thing in the morning. They wear white smocks without pockets. Their every move is recorded on video tape, and everything they say is picked up on audio tape. They must check their possessions outside the locked door before they walk in, and they are escorted in and out by a security guard. When Sharon Loman, a soft-counter at the Sahara, adds the figures together on her calculator, a video camera peers over her shoulder. She works in a room packed with money and dreams. Being inside the count room is like being in jail, except that the kind of time these guys are serving is measured in an hourly wage.

"The day goes by pretty fast," says Jerry Hengst, one of the Sahara soft-counters. "Isn't it amazing that a hotel owner can own these boxes and have money fall out that people have given him, and be able to pay people to count it for him? Must be nice owning a casino."

Behind the counters are rows and rows of boxes containing table winnings, all waiting to be tallied. They will take, for instance, all of the swing shift blackjack boxes and count them together, and then move onto the swing shift craps count. Then they will

repeat the process for the day and graveyard shifts, game by game, shift by shift.

The counting begins by choosing the shift, sorting the boxes for the games, and then dumping out the boxes onto the counting table. They separate the various denominations—$1, $5, $10, $20, $50, $100, and so on—and put them in piles.

The count is on.

The figures are added twice, by two different counters, to ensure accuracy; then they are fed into a computer and, eventually, sent up to top management, where they will set the tone for the day. A good win, and everybody's happy; a loss, and something's got to be done about those cheaters.

The Sahara soft-counters add up around $100,000 each morning (the same amount that soars through the hard-count room, on average) with really big money on big weekends—when the house can win something like $500,000 at the tables and slots, all of which is counted by the eight hands of the count room.

"This isn't money," says Sahara soft-counter Sharon Loman. "It's paper. My job is to just get it in the correct order and count it correctly and get the figures right."

bunch of small-time jokes," says veteran casino executive and syndicated gaming columnist Geno Munari. "He thinks the guy is making fun of him. That's where that theory comes from. It's an old-time thing we're trying to change. There's nothing wrong with being friendly and saying hello."

The greatest dealing job in town is working at Caesars. Getting hired there is like winning the million-dollar lottery or the grand prize on "The $64,000 Question." We're talking retirement, second home in the country, Cadillac in the garage. If you've got the Juice to get the job.

"You can only get a job there if you know somebody," says one Strip dice dealer. "It's not something you could just walk into. It's nepotism at its greatest."

"It's difficult to get a job here because we have literally no turnover," says Bill Bischoff of Caesars.

The dealers know they have the best job in town and they don't leave. I look for somebody who's had at least two years of experience under their belt at a respectable place and who hasn't jumped from job to job. Most of the time, somebody in the casino will know the applicant, and I'm sure that's where people say this is the Juice.

"The Juice factor is in any town," says Buddy Spach of the Stardust.

It's just more up-front here. If you're gonna have people that work for you in the gambling biz, you want to have people you know, because they're handling your money. A guy who works for me and handles money on the table handles more money than I do. So if we can get some kind of background on him or know him or know somebody who knows him, we're going to feel a lot more comfortable hiring him. As opposed to some guy walking in off the street who we don't know.

Bischoff says that, Juice aside, what he terms really important is years on the table. "The best dealers have experience dealing with the more significant customers," he says. "They don't get riled. Customers can sense when a dealer is nervous, and we don't want that to happen." But, hey, what's to be nervous about? On a Super Bowl or fight night at Caesars, a good dealer can pull in something like $15,000 in tips, which may be one reason a Caesars dealer isn't interested in quitting and going somewhere else.

One constant of the gambling biz over the years is the male domination of the industry. It is a man's world. Male gangsters created Las Vegas for the amusement of men who played serious games while the women yanked the slots. Men own and run the casinos. The pit bosses are men. The casino managers are always men. The only female faces working in the casino are dealers, cocktail waitresses, cigarette girls, and keno runners.

"I think things are changing," says Sue Lowden, a former Las Vegas TV anchorwoman who works at the Sahara and Hacienda with her husband, Sahara and Hacienda owner Paul.

> I see a lot of single professional women with lots of money coming to Las Vegas and enjoying themselves. The atmosphere is changing here. It's friendlier. Casino people are becoming more helpful; they're willing to teach people how to play new games.

The women are there on the floor all right. Just don't try to find any female casino executives.

When Nevada legalized gambling, casinos were called "gambling houses," and the theme was usually Wild Western. As the industry began to gain respectability in the 1960s and 1970s, with the entry of Howard Hughes, Kirk Kerkorian, and the Hilton Corporation, a new *corporate* name was given to gambling: gaming.

"There's nothing that makes Benny Binion madder—and I don't blame him—than when people call it the 'gaming business,'" says Benny's son Jack, who runs the Horseshoe.

> When I first got into the gambling business, it was definitely a kind of sub-society. It had its own jargon, there was a kind of a mystique, it was like being in show business. A guy says "I'm a dealer," and he took pride in that—other dealers would watch dealers that were real good and study their craft. Now, working at Bally's or Hilton or the Tropicana is like working at General Motors—it's like going to work at a factory. It used to be that people never would leave the gambling business. . . . It was kind of like "we" against "them."
>
> Now they want to call it the "gaming business." That's kind of like calling a whorehouse a brothel. People are still embarrassed by the word *gambling*. A brothel sounds better, but it's still going to be a whorehouse no matter what you call it.

"I came to Vegas in an $8,000 Cadillac and left in an $80,000 bus."

—Milton Berle

81

SUITES

"Presidential." "Villa." "Mrs. Miniver." Vegas suites. The pads where Sammy, Frank, and Dean snooze, Elvis and Priscilla honeymooned, and high rollers relax in the manner to which they are accustomed.

Home of giant Jacuzzis, round beds, gaudy wallpaper, lots of rooms, mirrors on the ceiling, many reflective surfaces, and excessive gadgetry.

Stars do sleep here, but the main function of the suite is to provide luxury accommodations for high rollers.

"The important thing is to give the gambler the feeling that an unlimited amount of money has been spent on him," says Donald Schmitt, who designed the suites for the MGM Grand (now Bally's). "The trick of good design is to be flamboyant, but not cheap."

What the high roller can choose from in suites:

• Great tubs: The "Island Theme" suite at the Tropicana has a giant rock-formation whirlpool tub in the middle of the room. Any suite at Caesars comes with a giant Jacuzzi.

The lavish Caesar's suites, in orange and red, with round beds, jacuzzis, and mirrored ceilings in every room

• Unforgettable upholstery: Cowhide and calfskin on Louis XIV dining room chairs in the "western" suite at the Las Vegas Hilton.

• Two floors: Most suites at the Golden Nugget and Caesars have winding staircases, with a lavish living room downstairs and a big bedroom upstairs.

• Big bathrooms: Most suites at Bally's (which are still named after MGM movies like *Mrs. Miniver* and *Ben-Hur*) feature a large white bathtub on a pedestal, surrounded by a French-style railing. Many expensive suites have a bidet next to the toilet bowl.

• Vast ceilings: For example, the coffered ceiling covered with beveled mirrors, surrounded by giant bamboo poles in the bedroom of the "Manchu" apartment at the Nugget.

"They are fantasies on a lot of levels," says Steve Wynn about the Golden Nugget suites. "We want them to look like a penthouse in New York would look if you could afford anything you ever dreamed of."

Caesars Olympic Tower suites look nothing like New York. They're as Vegas as they come. The suites are notable for the six-hundred-square-foot living room with winding Lucite staircase, the round bed with mirrored ceiling, and a round Jacuzzi set on a raised platform in front of two windows overlooking the Strip. The prevailing color of the rooms is red, because it suggests

"aggressive action," says Craig Beckstead of Franklin Design, who created them.

The Palace's fourteen Villa Suites (including "Antonius," "Augustus," "Caligula," "Claudius," "Julius," "Nero," "Remus," "Romulus," and "Titus") are furnished in an Art Deco—as opposed to early Roman—style and overlook the big, blue, 114-foot-long, 79-foot-wide swimming pool.

The Las Vegas Hilton's nine "classic suites" (with names like "The Gold Coast," "Hollywood," and "Desert") aren't really classic Vegas suites. Like those at the Nugget, they're more in line with the toniest New York homes.

"The Gold Coast" suggests the theme of the movie *Raiders of the Lost Ark*. It features 2,500 square feet filled with fantasy objects: an Egyptian-style bar with carved faux-granite sphinxes; imitation palm tree lighting fixtures; simulated rock tables; an elaborate front door carved with lion and elephant heads; and a leopard footstool next to a bed in simulated snakeskin. Says designer Zoli Kovacs: "Anything worth doing is worth overdoing."

"They're fabulous," Bill Cosby says of the new Hilton suites, "because they *do* get you away from naughtiness. In the old ones, the theme was naughty, a whole feeling of guilt." Cosby convinced the Hilton to redecorate the "Elvis" suite for him. "They got out of that red-and-black bordello look to something early American. It's gorgeous now."

"Fasten your money belts, we're
coming in for a landing."

—Don Rickles

CHAPTER 5

Casino Czars

Not every casino in Vegas is run by a big corporation like Hilton, Ramada, or Holiday Inn. Several still operate as in the old days—under one-man or family rule. Meet three such Vegas operators, the Binions of the Horseshoe, Steve Wynn of the Golden Nugget, and Paul and Sue Lowden of the Sahara and Hacienda.

Benny Binion, legendary patriarch of the Horseshoe Club

THE BINIONS

Where else but in Las Vegas would you find a "gambling house" started by a Texas gambler in 1942, where mother watches over the books, the two boys run the casino, and the grandson is a security guard?

It's Benny Binion's Horseshoe Club, the legendary institution where anyone can have their picture taken (for free) with $1,000,000 in $10,000-bills as a backdrop. Because of its reputation as "the gambler's gambling house," the Horseshoe is always packed. Saturday night, people stand in line waiting to get a seat at one of the blackjack tables. The dice tables, which feature ten times odds (instead of two times on the Strip) are also hopping.

The Horseshoe is a money machine. The top five casinos in Vegas are Caesars Palace, the Las Vegas Hilton, Bally's, the Flamingo Hilton, and Circus Circus—all places with two to three thousand rooms, giant parking lots, shows, tour groups, and high rollers who fly in from all over the world to spend money there. In sixth place is the diminutive Horseshoe, which collects nearly $300,000,000 in gamblers' losses each year. How do they do it? Volume, volume, volume.

Binion's Horseshoe is a place of smoke in the air, cocktail waitresses with gartered thighs, and noise. The only music you'll hear is the sound of coins falling from the slots, jackpot bells ringing, and the p.a. droning: "Paging Mr. Binion. Phone call for Jack Binion." (Jack runs the entire operation; his brother Ted is in charge of the casino.)

Horseshoe high rollers aren't upper-class millionaires from Saudi Arabia and Korea. No, these are guys out of Damon Runyon, characters with names like Puggy, Silent Harry, and Texas Dolly.

"What makes the place so successful is that Benny understands what it is that makes his customers tick," says Steve Wynn of the Golden Nugget. "At the Nugget we try to make everything beautiful. We buy jets, limos, helicopters . . . the Horseshoe puts it all into the casino. They just happen to have a hotel upstairs."

"They're nice clean rooms," says Benny Binion, "not luxury, but as clean as can be. There's none cleaner."

Just don't try to book one.

"We don't take any reservations," he says. "If I know you, you got a room, but if I don't, you don't get a room. If you walked in off the street, you'd have to call somebody I knew to get you in."

Gambler Benny Binion left Texas after indictment on two murder raps (one earned him a two-year suspended sentence, the other charge was dismissed) and came to Las Vegas in 1951, where he took over the El Dorado Hotel, re-christening it the Horseshoe. It was the first downtown gambling house to put carpets on the floor.

85

A Sahara change person

Besides the rugs, Binion had two other calling cards: money and no limits.

He had noticed the crowds of people in Washington, D.C., standing in line at the Bureau of Printing and Engraving just to look at the big bucks, and he figured they'd like to have their picture taken in front of $1,000,000. It was a good publicity stunt that still works today. But, more importantly, Binion's attracts the gamblers, big and small, because there are no table limits. You can bet anything you want at Binion's gambling house. (Most places won't accept wagers over $1,000 to $5,000 for fear of breaking their bank.)

One gambler walked calmly into the Horseshoe on an afternoon and plunked $777,000 on the craps table. He threw the dice once and walked away with $1,500,000. The sad part of this story is that he returned five months later, put $1,000,000 down on the table, and, with a single throw of the dice, lost it all.

Some famous Benny Binion stories:

One day in the 1950s, Binion became suspicious of a man at the craps table who kept his money close to his sleeves. The man became hysterical after he lost $11,000. Binion called him into his office to find out what troubled the fellow, whereupon the man explained to Binion that he was a Baptist minister back East and now he didn't know whether he should go back and repent to the congregation or not. Binion said: "I tell you what I'm going to do, I'm going to give you back $1,000 and you better not go back and tell the congregation. The Lord will forgive you, but the congregation won't." A year later Binion received a $1,000 check from the temporarily wild gambling pastor.

Then there was the incident in Binion's restaurant. A man walked in and ate $26 worth of food, then marched up to Binion, announced that he didn't have a dime to his name, and asked to be arrested. Binion didn't want the guy to spend the night in jail only to be let out the next day.

So I said, "Let's fix his business up." It was cold as hell, so I took everything off him but his shorts and threw him on the street. He never dreamed anything like that would happen. If he had eaten $6 worth of food, it wouldn't have bothered me. But it takes a lot to eat $26 worth of food—alone.

The Wild, Wild West is still alive and well at the Horseshoe, which has no hosts to take care of the gamblers and no computers to keep track of the players.

"We don't want the government tracking our players," says Jack Binion. "We don't want to track him. This," he says, pointing to his head, "is our computer."

Part of the charm of the Horseshoe is the Wild West atmosphere, with Benny Binion as the crotchety Walter Brennan type. Ask him, and he'll freely tell you about his troubles with the law. A 1950s income tax charge? A set-up. The Texas murder raps? Self-defense, at least one of them anyway. "A guy shot at me. I shot back. He missed. I didn't." Then he'll also tell you that he "ain't got too much respect for the law. They don't conduct themselves to have respect. I know too much about 'em."

Dealers taking a break in their lounge at Binion's Horseshoe

Nor have legal troubles hurt Binion's. Business is booming—in 1988 the Binions bought the Mint Hotel and Casino nextdoor, which means there's more room at the tables: even more important, if you want to make a room reservation, Binion's can now comply.

The house mascot still is Benny: go to the Horseshoe restaurant and get the "Benny Binion Natural"—steak and eggs for $1.99—or "Binion's Delight," the classic Binion burger.

Want to find the Binions? All you have to do is walk into the coffee shop around lunch time and you'll probably find most of them at the "Binion" table—the one in the middle of the room, closest to the kitchen. That's the office for the casino, where the Binions meet every day to discuss business. When lunch is over, wife Teddy Jane will probably be going to the count room with daughters Barbara and Becky to tally the receipts, and sons Jack and Ted will go to the casino to tend to business.

Teddy Jane lives in a hotel room upstairs; Benny spends most of his time on a ranch in Pahrump, Nevada, and in Montana. The rest of the clan lives near the gambling house.

"I'll tell you," says Benny Binion, "I ain't a smart guy . . . I never did go to school. I'm just a gambler, and a darn ignorant one at that."

But he must have done something right. Down the street from the Horseshoe, on Ogden and Casino Center boulevards, there is a nine-foot statue of Benny Binion riding a horse. It is the only statue in Nevada honoring a gambler.

In 1988, the statue was unveiled the day the family put up their new neon sign. They bought the Mint, their nextdoor neighbor, and expanded their operation into the place, becoming one whole block long in the process. There's now more room at the tables, and even more importantly, if you want to make a room reservation, Binion's can now comply.

STEVE WYNN

If Benny Binion represents the old Las Vegas, Steve Wynn is the image of the new. Wynn is tall; Binion is short. Binion wears western shirts with gold coins in place of the buttons; Wynn wears the finest high-fashion designs. Yet both are gamblers out of the old Damon Runyon school, Binion just does it like a cowboy, and Wynn like a yuppie.

Wynn brings to his properties sophistication, bluntness, and a politician's zeal for promotion. Like Binion, he came into town with virtually nothing to his name (well, okay, $10,000) and turned the Golden Nugget into one of the biggest forces in Vegas.

"I was first here in 1952 when I was ten years old," says Wynn.

There was nothing but desert in between the Frontier and the Dunes. I used to go horseback riding every day in the sand. Everybody was wearing cowboy boots and hats. It was glamorous, it had stars, it had the Mafia. Nobody knew who was who.

I looked at the pit bosses, who wore those high collars . . . and the cocktail waitresses, who were all very beautiful, and I said to myself, what a hell of a business! I was intrigued by a business that offered the glamour of the movies and the stability of a bank.

As he got older, Wynn worked with his father in their chain of Maryland bingo parlors and moved to Vegas in 1967, where he tried to invest his own $10,000 plus $25,000 he had raised in the Frontier Hotel. The Nevada Gaming Commission put a stop to that, not because of Wynn, but because of some alleged underworld ownership that was part of the deal. Howard Hughes bought the hotel instead.

Wynn met E. Parry Thomas, head of the Valley Bank, who helped him acquire a liquor distributorship. With profits from that, Thomas helped Wynn buy a prime piece of real estate: a small parking lot next to Caesars Palace. Wynn threatened to open a casino there and sold the land back to Caesars for $2,000,000. With that bankroll, he invested in the Golden Nugget in 1969.

The Nugget had opened in 1946 as the first strictly gambling venture in the state—all tables and slots, no rooms. When Wynn got there, there was still no hotel—just a small, historic downtown gambling house with some tables, wheels, and slots.

Steve Wynn, the new breed of
Vegas mogul

The new Golden Nugget under construction—on the Strip

89

The old Golden Nugget—downtown

Wynn increased his stake in the Nugget and got a board seat in 1973. He was able to take control of the company that year when he discovered that some employees were skimming profits. Then it was on to Atlantic City, where he spent $8,500,000 for a motel, tore it down, and built the five-hundred-room Golden Nugget of Atlantic City. It opened in 1980 and quickly became one of the most profitable hotels on the Boardwalk. One year it made nearly $200,000,000 in profits.

He invested those profits in rebuilding the downtown Vegas Nugget, changing its image from a downtown gambling hall to a classy resort for the affluent.

"The Nugget proved you could get a better class of people downtown," says Wynn. "All the people who stay here used to stay on the Strip. We didn't steal the customers from the Mint or the Fremont."

Wynn was attracting high rollers in Atlantic City and low rollers in downtown Vegas, but he wanted to be consistent in the company.

> In order to get the people to stay here, you've got to make it the sort of place they want it to be. How do you get them in, so that everyone else wants to be around them? I figured let's fix the whole place up, change the outside, and tell everybody that we're fancy.

And that he did. He changed the face of downtown Vegas. For the new look, the hotel with the most-photographed neon sign in town became the first (and still the only) Vegas gambling establishment *without* a large neon sign. There was, indeed, nothing garish about the new Nugget on the street they call Glitter Gulch. It is understated white with imported palm trees.

But his plans didn't stop downtown. In 1987 he announced his intention to build the biggest, most elaborate resort on the Strip. The first new hotel on the Strip since the MGM Grand in 1972, Wynn's $550,000,000 resort—called the Mirage—is scheduled to open in late 1989 with over three thousand rooms and palm trees and waterfalls galore.

"They don't need another casino in Las Vegas, but they sure as hell could use a major attraction here," says Wynn, who also says that his new resort is to Vegas what Disneyland is to Anaheim. "It just happens to have a casino attached."

To raise funds for the new casino, Wynn sold the Atlantic City operation to Bally's for $450,000,000. The Mirage is strategically located next to Caesars—its biggest competitor for the high-roller trade—and across the street from the Flamingo Hilton and Bally's.

Wynn's decision to build the Mirage on the Strip had a ripple effect throughout town: the Flamingo Hilton, Holiday Casino, Imperial Palace, Sahara, and the Dunes all announced expansion programs, and Circus Circus announced plans to build a new gambling castle—Excalibur—on the other side of the street.

"The Strip," says Wynn, "is now the center of the universe. I feel like a new anchor of a major shopping center. And who's going to be the net donor and receiver of humans? If this was your place, would you be worried about the flow of traffic? Do you think the people staying in my hotel will be running [across the street] to the Holiday [casino]? No. They're going to have to come and see it [the Mirage]."

One of the town's biggest boosters, Wynn says Vegans shouldn't be so uptight about their town's gangster image:

> To the average person, organized crime as it related to Las Vegas was part of the show. They were like celebrities. . . . The mystique of it is all over. We've been trying to deny our heritage and history for so long, and so vigorously, every once in a while I wake up and realize we're shooting ourselves in the foot. Let America think what it wants about Las Vegas and shut up.

PAUL AND SUE LOWDEN

Paul Lowden left Wilmington, Delaware, in 1965 with nothing but a suitcase, $7,500 in his pocket, and a Hammond B-3 organ in a U-Haul.

Today he owns the Sahara and Hacienda hotels, which make more money in an hour than he ever saw in a night when his trio played the lounges.

Lowden came to Vegas for the same reason everyone else comes: "The money was good," says Lowden.

Paul and Sue Lowden in a suite at their Sahara Hotel: he came to Vegas in 1965 with his Hammond B-3 organ in a U-Haul, acquired 15 percent of the Hacienda in 1972, the rest of it in 1976, and the Sahara in 1982.

Placing the bet

There wasn't a lot of work in Wilmington. To have an organ in Las Vegas was to have an instrument that was always in demand. It had a sound, a certain sound. It was the days of the Jimmy Smith Trio. He was an idol of mine. He used to attack the instrument like Bud Powell attacked the piano.

While working the lounges, Lowden started making extra money in the business end of the music business—handling payroll, contracting for orchestras, putting acts together for other lounges. He started investing in the stock market; he recalls playing the organ with a copy of the *Wall Street Journal* next to him. The Flamingo Hilton hired him as entertainment director in 1970; he went to the Hacienda in 1972 and at the same time was able to purchase 15 percent of the hotel for $250,000, with a $125,000 loan from E. Parry Thomas's Valley Bank.

Making the switch wasn't hard. The gambling business is "very similar to other businesses," says Lowden. "It's a people business. Basically, you're dealing with a commodity. The house holds a certain percentage. There are little quirks, like knowing how much credit to give a person. . . ."

He didn't leave entertainment behind completely; he started a personal management firm with promoter Bernie Yuman. The deal was that Lowden would finance the company and Yuman would run it. It turned out to be one of his greatest investments. Yuman—who had been representing Wayne Cochran and the C. C. Riders—signed up two German magicians who had been working cruise ships and had just gotten a small job in a show at the MGM Grand. Siegfried and Roy went on to become two of the hottest stars in town, their *Beyond Belief* show at the Frontier selling out every performance for seven years running. Yuman negotiated a five-year, $57,500,000 deal for the two magicians to play the new Golden Nugget on the Strip beginning in 1989. Lowden gets 50 percent of the management fee, which has been estimated at $50,000 a month.

Lowden bought the entire Hacienda in 1977 for the fire-sale price of $21,000,000 (of which only $1,500,000 was his; the rest was from Valley Bank)—after state investigators discovered that majority owner Allen Glick had been skimming some $7,000,000 in coins from the Hacienda, Stardust, Fremont, and Marina hotels since 1974.

The Hacienda was a good deal, but the deal for the purchase of the Sahara was even better. It is one of the Strip's best locations (across the street from the convention center and Circus Circus), and Lowden got it for a song—just $50,000,000. The purchase price was raised on Wall Street by a publicly traded limited partnership—a first in the gambling industry.

"They say we stole the Sahara for $50,000,000," declares Lowden. "But we did have to invest another $2,500,000 for new slots, then put in our own bankroll in the cage, and cover the marker floats, and that was another $5,000,000." Finally, Lowden spent another $10,000,000 building a 575-room, 26-story tower to bring the Sahara's room count up to 1,500.

In contrast to such hardened cookies as Binion or brash operators like Steve Wynn, Lowden—a born-again Christian—is as down to earth and personable as they come. But faced with such an incredible rags-to-riches story, some of his critics charge that something's got to be wrong. Since he was once partnered with Glick, "the boys" (they say) must be financing him. Lowden says it simply isn't true—he owes his success solely to the fact that he has made good investments.

Lowden runs the Sahara and Hacienda with second wife Sue, a former local TV news anchor. She helps out with publicity and marketing and produces the in-house videos that teach guests how to gamble. Son Chris (from a previous marriage) is the maître d' at the Hacienda.

"Paul is extremely bright," says Sue. "He's a determined workaholic. You've also got to say he's been very lucky."

Paul met Sue when he called her up at the TV station and asked her for a date.

Contemplation

He said he'd been watching me and detected a New Jersey accent and thought that we should meet. As I was talking to him on the telephone, my assignment editor came up to me with a yellow pad and wrote, "Accept the date and find out when he's buying the Sahara"·in big yellow letters.

Nine months later, they were married, both for the second time. (He bought the hotel about a year after their date.)

Marrying into the gambling business gave Sue a different perspective on Las Vegas life. As a reporter, she would look forward to a big convention coming to town—lots of big stories. But her husband wouldn't be happy about the coming influx of delegates. "He'd say it was a working convention, and the delegates wouldn't be using the [gambling] tables as much as people who are here on vacation."

At home, Paul Lowden practices the organ every day. "His favorite line is that he never knows if he's going to need a job," says Sue. He occasionally plays some tunes in the lounges of the Hacienda and Sahara; he plays hymns at church every Sunday.

"I really do miss the organ," he says.

I think if I could do that for a living, I'd probably still be doing it, but it was something that evolved. There's limited opportunities. Even if you're the best—which I was not— you're still playing lounges and fighting owners. But I still practice.

CHAPTER 6
Games Gamblers Play

SLOTS

$1,500,000,000 was lost on the 62,000 slot machines in Clark County in 1987.

No game produces more revenue in Vegas. That's why most of the casinos in town now are the so-called grind joints. They appeal to the small bettors, who like to pour their coins into the one-armed bandits all day.

But while slots may be the most popular game in town, if you're looking for a good return on your money, table games are a better investment. "Table games keep 35¢–37¢ on the dollar," says Tropicana Hotel vice president Butch Witcher, "while slots keep 75¢–78¢ on the dollar."

The signs everywhere in Vegas say something different: LOOSE SLOTS—97.5% PAYBACK. What exactly does that mean?

"At least one machine in the casino will pay back 98 percent," says Geno Munari, a casino executive at the Marina who also writes a syndicated gaming column for several newspapers and magazines.

But there's never a way to figure out which one it is.

Loose slot is a generic term used to convince you that a particular casino is a great place to play. A good example of a place *not* to play is at the airport or a 7-Eleven. A local place that thrives on repeat business is going to have to have a liberal machine, because they want the customer to return. At the airport, it's transit trade—do they really care if the customer ever comes back?

Munari adds that the "loose" slot of the house will always be placed in between two "tight" slots, meaning that folks in search of jackpots should look for winning machines and wait for the player to walk away from it before dropping coins.

The slot machine was invented in San Francisco in 1895 by Charles Fey. His prototype was the "Liberty Bell," a nickel slot that awarded 10¢ for two bells, $1 dollar for three. The slot was a staple of early San Francisco saloons and most twentieth-century casinos; however, it was a small-time amusement relegated to the back of the room.

"We were always second-rate citizens," says Witcher, vice president of slot operations at the Tropicana. "Right now, we've finally overcome the Rodney Dangerfield syndrome. We're finally starting to get some respect." The turning point, he says, was the introduction of gambling in Atlantic City, where new casino executives came to work unprejudiced about slots. "The owners and general managers were all fairly new to the business," he says. "They didn't know slots were second class. They just started looking at the numbers and found that slots were pulling in major revenue."

In Vegas, what helped slots finally overtake table games in 1984 was the introduction of the dollar slot machine. The bigger investment meant bigger potential payoffs—as well as player losses and, therefore, huge wins for the house. At the $1 slot, most players risk $2 or $3 (the same as the minimum at the twenty-one table) trying for the $10,000 to $1,000,000 jackpot.

The Mills Baseball Vendor, a slot machine from 1929. The reel strip symbols included baseball gloves, bats, bases, balls; the machine could be played by *two* players, who used the outcome of the reels to determine hits and position of men on the bases.

OPPOSITE:
The latest look in slots

But the casinos haven't stopped with the buck slots. Caesars and the Hilton have $5, $25, and even $100 slot machines. Indeed, casino marketing is now oriented toward the slot player. Today, "Bally's Is Slots," "The Tropicana Pays More Jackpots," Fitzgerald's is the home of "Nevada's Loosest Slots," and the slots of the Sahara have "More Payoffs."

Casinos regularly host "slot tournaments," in which couples pay an up-front fee—like $1,000—in exchange for three days of room, food, and beverage, and the chance to pull slot arms eight hours a day. No coins drop out. Instead, players accumulate points. The player with the highest score at the end of the weekend wins the grand prize—which is usually something like $10,000 or $20,000.

Aside from the tourneys, at which the slot player is wined and dined, the "serious" slot player can also secure complimentary privileges. Witcher considers a "medium serious" slot player someone who will drop $500–$2,000 worth of $1 tokens in the slots over a weekend. A "top notch" slot player is someone parting with $10,000.

The Trop, like other casinos, issues house credit cards that can be inserted into the slot. The machine keeps track of how much time the player has spent on the game, information that determines what kind of comps he gets—a free room or a free room, food, and beverage.

"I'm not interested in whether they win or lose," says Witcher. "Just give me your action. Come in and play." His only other criterion is that a "good" slot player isn't playing the nickels or quarters. It's got to be dollars.

Even though slots are generally a bad investment for the gambler, more good news comes out about slot winners than winners of any other form of gaming. You never hear about the $25,000 blackjack winner, but you can regularly learn about folks who win $10,000, $20,000, and $100,000 on slots. The Las Vegas Hilton, the Golden Nugget, and Caesars have had several winners on their million-dollar slots. Megabucks, a statewide string of slots all tied to the same system, lottery-fashion, had a $6,900,000 winner in 1988, the biggest slot jackpot in history.

Howard Sorkazian, a Los Angeles auto mechanic, came to the Las Vegas Hilton one day

Jackpot winners from the Hilton

in 1985, invested $3 and won $250,000. He returned in 1987, put in another $3 and this time won $2,100,000 from the Hilton's "Pot O' Gold" slots. The hotel gave him a big check and a silver "7777" pin. He quit his job, opened up his own body shop, and now returns to the Hilton twice a month to play the machines. "The people that say you can't win on slots are wrong," he says. "The best way to make money in Vegas is on the machines." (The biggest Vegas slot winner, as of 1988, is Florida truck driver Vernon Renfro, who walked away from the Golden Nugget with $3,000,000.)

The slots have graduated from the bells and fruit of earlier days to BAR—BAR—BAR, 7—7—7—7, and video screens. Most casinos have modern slots like video poker or video "reels" to satisfy the American consumer, who is comfortable sitting in front of the tube. And nothing looks more like a TV set than the video poker machine, another relatively recent addition to the boom in slots. Here is a machine that doesn't require mindless dropping of coins and pulling of handles; it's a video game featuring the favorite adult pasttime: cards. Drop a quarter in the machine and get your five cards, discard as many as you like, and hope you get two pairs, three- or four-of-a-kind, a straight, or a flush. "I'm hooked on video poker, I play it every night," says Bobby Berosini, who does an act with orangutans in the *Lido de Paris* show at the Stardust. "It's a visual thing, and I'm a visual guy. It's like playing solitaire. It's not like playing a slot, because you're constantly making decisions."

Munari says the best slot bets in town are the big jackpots and video poker. The poker machines to look for are the ones with the highest payoffs (payoffs are conveniently listed on the front). For flushes and full houses, the most a machine will pay is nine coins for one coin invested; other machines pay back five or six coins. Munari also says nickel and quarter machines keep more money than the dollar slot—the best ones to play, he says.

BJ

Some $540,700,000 was lost on the 1,900 blackjack tables in Clark County in 1987. The odds against the player: 3 percent, which means that if one hundred hands of twenty-one were dealt, the player would win 47 and the house would win 53.

Gaming expert Geno Munari and
Pamela Collins at the blackjack table

Hit me.
Stand.
Bust.
Blackjack!

It's the language of Nevada's most popular table game—twenty-one, or blackjack. It's
the game new gamblers turn to and veterans enjoy for the same reason: the rules are incredibly
simple. It's player versus dealer, each attempting to get a hand as close to twenty-one as
possible, without going over that mark.

"Twenty-one is a rapid and simple game," says Munari. "People think they can beat it.
There's a skill involved and participation. The reason it makes so much money for the house is
that players have to act [with bets] before the dealer does." That is, the player bets before he
knows what his cards will be, unlike the poker player, who can raise his bet *after* he sees his
cards.

Players who read up on the "counting" systems developed by mavens like Edward Thorpe
and Ken Uston can learn methods to help make twenty-one pay off. Of all the games, study
in this one can result in the player coming out ahead.

Sammy Davis, Jr., has been playing the game since 1958, when the Sands opened its
casino to blacks. He usually loses more than he wins, but he still likes to play anyhow. When
Davis performs at Bally's, $2,000 in credit is available for his use at the twenty-one tables.

Maybe I'll play, maybe I won't, but it's my favorite game. The fun of the cards going
back and forth. It's the last of the gentlemen's games. Dice is too physical, all that
yelling and screaming. You can still sit with a gold cigarette case at a blackjack table
and play. It still smacks of James Bond.

More Bondian devices pop up in the game of blackjack than any other table game.
Twenty-one is the game cheaters like most, and it has the greatest variety of scams associated
with it. For example: bending a card or marking it in some other way to remember its value
when it comes back up through the deck; joining forces with the dealer and working out eye
and face signals when certain cards come up; palming aces in coat or shirt sleeves. Most casinos
use four to six decks of cards in twenty-one to minimize the possibility of the player hitting

blackjack. Munari says that anytime you can find a casino dealing one- or two-deck twenty-one (and there are some), take advantage of it.

Twenty-one is the game dealers begin with when they start their careers, but it's not a job that makes for a pleasant existence.

"They're never happy, because they get it from both sides," says Tropicana vice president Butch Witcher. "If the player is losing money, he's upset but the house is happy; and if the player is winning, he's happy but the house is mad."

It's eight hours a day of shuffling, dealing, picking up chips, exchanging cash for chips, and clapping your hands before you go on a break—to show the eye-in-the-sky security system that you are not walking away with any pilfered bucks.

"When you first start out at it, it's an exciting job," says Stardust twenty-one dealer Sharon Rennie, "but then after a while it just becomes like any other job. It pays the bills and takes care of the kids. What else can I say?"

Joan Spaulding was a secretary at the Las Vegas Hilton and asked to be a twenty-one

Hilton twenty-one dealer Joan Spaulding

dealer because she was tired of sitting behind a desk all day. "I'd rather stand all day than sit." When she started dealing, she found herself dreaming about cards when she slept. "I'd see cards in my eyes, I'd hear 'change $100' or 'cut' and 'shuffle.' . . . Eventually, I grew out of it."

Within an hour, an average of sixty hands of blackjack will be dealt. Spaulding and Rennie get one twenty-minute break per hour, which means they'll deal forty hands an hour—or 320 hands a day. Believe it or not, after all those hands, Spaulding occasionally goes out after work and partakes in the game as a player.

"I play by the book," she says, "but it is all luck. If the dealer has a ten, you should always hit to seventeen, even at sixteen. Those are the rules."

Spaulding and Rennie, like all dealers, make their living from tips, which are split among all the dealers at the casino on a twenty-four-hour basis. "Some people are good with tips, some people just don't tip at all," says Rennie. "It kind of gets you when they win thousands of dollars, but what are you going to do? I've seen people go into a restaurant where they don't tip the waitress or cocktail waitress. That's just their character. Some people just aren't tippers."

What's not in Rennie's character is talking. She likes to keep to herself. "I try to be nice, but there are days when you just don't feel like talking to people; that's true in any job."

CRAPS

Some $289,000,000 was lost on the 262 crap tables in Clark County in 1987. Odds against the player: 1.404 percent on the Don't Pass line and 1.441 percent on the Pass line. The odds mean the house is likely to win 51 out of 100 games.

Craps is the game of the traditional gambler, the sport Nathan Detroit and Nicely-Nicely Johnson enjoyed in *Guys and Dolls*, the game the Vegas gangsters who built the town liked to play. "Most guys learned to play craps in the Army, and there aren't a lot of street corners left in the city, either," says Sahara casino manager John Boni. "That's where they learned to play dice. It's basically a game that tends to be played by the older generation. The younger players tend to play twenty-one."

But craps is *the* game to play if you want to win some money.

There is no short way to explain the rules of craps. It's a dice game with seven different ways to bet. Basically, the player shoots the dice and hopes to come up with a seven or an eleven. But there is more.

The Pass Line and Don't Pass Line

Two of the best bets in the gambling house, according to Munari, are money on the Pass or Don't Pass line, both holding about a 1 percent advantage for the casino. Roll a seven or an eleven on a Pass line bet and you get even money; roll a two, three, or twelve and you "crap out." If any other number comes up, say a four, you get a point and roll again. You can roll as many times as you want to in search of the four—as long as a seven doesn't come up. If it does, you lose.

Don't Pass is almost the opposite. Throwing a seven or eleven on the first roll is an automatic loss; a throw of a two or three is a win. A first roll of twelve is a push and nobody wins.

Come

This wager is the same as a bet on the Pass line, except that it is placed after the first roll or on any following roll.

Don't Come

Similar to Don't Pass, the Don't Come bet is placed after the first roll of the dice.

Field

A bet for one roll only. The field consists of seven numbers—two, three, four, nine, ten, eleven, and twelve. If any of these numbers is thrown, the player wins even money, except for two and twelve, which pay two to one.

The Big Six and Eight

An even-money bet, which wins if a total of six or eight is rolled.

Any Seven

A payoff of five for one if a seven is thrown on the first roll. So a bet of $100 would garner $400 back.

"Craps," says Munari, "is one of the most exciting games in the casino. You get to throw the dice, there's a lot of yelling, a lot of action, and there's lots of different things to do."

Craps is also one of the more fun games to deal.

"I liken dealing twenty-one to screwing in bolts eight hours a day at General Motors," says Caesars Palace dice dealer Jess Hammond. "Dice is more exciting. There's more things to do. You don't just stand there and shuffle cards."

"It's more involved, more complicated," says Stardust dice dealer Howard Ritchie. "Twenty-one is boring, and people take it personally when they lose the money. In the dice pit it's

Dice dealer Howard Ritchie at the Stardust

Craps

totally opposite. The player knows we have no control over the dice. If the dice doesn't come out right, there's nothing they can do."

The biggest mistake dice players make at the tables?

"They don't go home when they should," says Hammond. "That's why we're a city without clocks. When people can't see outside and can't see the sun come up, they have a tendency to play sixteen to eighteen hours at a stretch, because they're all hyped up and excited. They should be calling it a night."

Hammond on dice dealing:

> For a guy with no higher education, I've turned out to be a pretty good mathematician. My job starts with getting along with people and being able to do numbers in my head and knowing what the various payoffs are. It can get pretty hectic here. We have more of the carriage trade, wealthy people with more money to bet, which means you have to be that much better of a dealer. It requires a little more knowledge than the average casino dealer because you're dealing in such large sums.
>
> The trick is being around long enough so that when one giant pile of chips gets placed before your eyes, you can handle it and not get flustered. Once my eyes just bulged open and my mind went totally blank. Somebody asked me my name and I couldn't tell them. That's how flustered I was.

Ritchie's tense day was the time a guy keeled over and died at the dice table. "But they just kept the game going right along," he says. "They don't stop for nothing."

BACCARAT

Some $151,500,000 was lost on the fifty-four baccarat tables in Clark County in 1987. Like craps, the game has a 1.2 to 1.3 percent advantage for the house.

Baccarat is one of the oldest games in the world. It goes way back to 1490 and the reign of Charles VIII, when it became the favorite game of French nobility. Europe's most popular casino game, baccarat is what James Bond plays in Monte Carlo and the super high rollers play in Las Vegas. At Caesars Palace, rollers have been known to walk away with—or drop—two or three or four big ones, which in Vegas means millions.

"Everybody knows about them; that's common conversation in Las Vegas," says Sahara casino manager John Boni. "Everybody here has dreams of being what we call a Friday-night millionaire."

Unlike virtually every other game in the house, baccarat is set up for spectators. At Caesars, the pit is right next to the Circus Maximus show room, with a railing for people to lean on as they watch the four games unfolding in the pit.

The object of the card game is to come as close as possible to the number nine. In baccarat scoring, card hands are totaled, but only the last digit is used. (For example, 10 plus 5 equals 15, but the score is 5.)

Dealers in the Caesars baccarat pit come to work every morning with a big smile. The baccarat pit is where the really big players ("whales," as they are known at Caesars) play, and

Robert Barragan, manager of the "friendliest baccarat game in town" at the Sahara

Caesars Palace baccarat dealer Eddie Borla

the potential toke haul for the dealer is unlimited. When things get heavy, the game sometimes has a $10,000 minimum—*per hand*, just to play. The only negative is that the whales can be rather testy as they lose. One morning at eight in the Caesars baccarat pit, two Asian players were slouched at the table with lousy cards and nasty expressions. The atmosphere could be best described as tense, with poker-faced, bow-tied baccarat dealer Eddie Borla keeping his mouth shut and dealing cards as the players got more and more upset. The pit was empty, save for the one table with the two players, Borla, and the baccarat manager. I was told that the two whales had been there since eight P.M. the night before and were on a bad losing streak—some $500,000 each had been lost so far.

No game keeps more cash on hand than baccarat, as I was to learn the morning I came to photograph Borla. Caesars asked me to come early, presumably before the whales arrived. But since the two high rollers were already there, I asked if they would mind if I moved Borla to a table on the other side of the room to take his picture. Yes, they would mind, it would be distracting. So I went to a private casino next to the Caesars Bacchanal restaurant, where a table was set up, and chips were brought in. The cage cashier arrived with the normal amount of baccarat chips: $750,000.

And the two whales? They ended up at six P.M. one million dollars in the hole. But, hey, they got a free room and all the free drinks they wanted while they played.

Borla joined the world of baccarat in 1981 after six years of dealing twenty-one. Prior to his gaming career he taught for many years at Vegas's only Catholic high school, Bishop Gorman, where he served as head of the business department, assistant athletic director, head baseball coach, assistant football coach, and taught five classes. He made $14,000 a year.

"The monetary value wasn't there," says Borla. "It was a great injustice. I felt I could do better."

Now Borla goes to work every day at four-thirty A.M., while his former Bishop Gorman colleagues are still fast asleep. He leaves work at twelve-thirty P.M., while they are eating lunch. He doesn't work the busiest baccarat shift of the day—that would be swing (six P.M. to two A.M.)—but it's a shift he finds easy to live with. "It works out well for my family," he says. "I don't need much sleep. If we go out in the evening, I can always sleep in the afternoon. I can function with three or four good hours of sleep."

Borla likes baccarat "because of the communication you can get with the customers. You can get more on a personal note than you can with any of the other games." The reason dealing baccarat at Caesars is one of the great casino jobs in Vegas is because "we're dealing with a larger volume," he says. "We deal from $20 minimum to $100,000 maximum. And, believe it or not, Mr. and Mrs. Joe America do come to play baccarat. They see the James Bond movies and they want to experience that, too."

(The last thing in the world any Vegas dealer ever wants to discuss is his salary, fearing the IRS will come and raid his home. But word around town is that big baccarat dealers tend to make $60,000 to $75,000 a year.)

Baccarat has always been the game of big money. It was played on a cash-only basis until 1974, when it converted to chips. Even though the big stack of bucks isn't there anymore, spectators know what a big stack of Caesars pink-and-brown chips mean: they are the largest denomination in town, worth $10,000 per chip.

Caesar's, Bally's, the Golden Nugget, and the Las Vegas Hilton have elaborate baccarat pits. However, the game isn't a ritzy $100,000-a-hand affair at every house in town. The Frontier and Flamingo Hilton deal baccarat at a table that looks just like a blackjack table (the only difference is the color of the felt). And then there's the $5 minimum game at the Sahara, which is "the friendliest in town" (or at least, so it says on the marquee).

"Most people are intimidated by the game at the other hotels," says Sahara baccarat manager Robert Barragan.

It's a cold atmosphere. Instead of being so stuffy and so quiet, we treat everybody here on a first-name basis. We make everyone feel like part of the family. Playing here is like walking into a living room.

We try to make it fun and exciting. If you win, it's exciting; if you lose, it's not that exciting. But even if you lose, you can have fun at the same time.

Rules in place at Caesars and Bally's—for example, cards must be dealt standing instead of sitting—are thrown out the window at the "friendliest" game. "There's no reason for that," says Barragan. "Sit down. Be comfortable. Relax. Talk among yourselves. Have a good time."

To hook people on the game, Barragan teaches baccarat every afternoon and gives students a bunch of no-value chips to play with. They end up returning in the evening. Just like the Caesars whales, players at the "friendliest baccarat game in town" have also been known to sit at the tables for a twenty-four-hour stretch and walk away, minus or plus $200,000.

"This is the adult Disneyland here," says Barragan. "And we're the greatest roller coaster ride in town. You're either up or you're down."

KENO

Some $79,000,000 was lost in the seventy-four keno rooms in Clark County in 1987. House advantage: 25 percent.

Whenever you go in the casinos, you can't help noticing on the walls the large boards with numbers. They're in all the restaurants and bars, as well as the keno pit. If you don't see the numbers on the wall, you surely will see the scantily-clad woman who walks up and down the casino saying, "Keno. Keno. Keno."

Keno is a game of Chinese origin that is the flip side of bingo. The rules are simple: twenty numbers are on a keno ticket; eighty randomly selected balls with numbers on them are pulled by the keno department; the player predicts—up to fifteen—which of the twenty will be picked. Keno has the worst odds in the house—25 percent against the player—but it's easy, and the potential winning from a $2 or $5 ticket is as high as $50,000.

"It's basically a game just for relaxation and killing time," says Pamela Preston, a keno runner at the Las Vegas Hilton, "to play in the coffee shop and continue gambling as you're eating."

Keno runners like Preston get to pick up all the keno tickets for the ten-minute games and then return the winning and losing tickets to the players after the game.

Over and over again.

Left: Bally's keno runner Kim Pepe;
right: Dawn Hale of the Riviera

The good keno runner needs a winning personality and an excellent memory. "And you've got to be pretty fast," says Riviera runner Dawn Hale. "We run the games ten minutes apart here, so I've got to move. They call for us all over. If they want me at the bar, at the coffee shop, at a blackjack table, at a craps table, I've got to be there."

Keno, along with roulette and slots, has historically been a game for women, but lately men have been enjoying it as well. "They like to meet the little keno runner," says Susan Cuellar, a Bally's runner.

We're a lot prettier to look at than the male roulette dealer. We don't let them get depressed. We always try to get their spirits up. We always tell them that if they're not winning here at this game, there's always another game in the casino for them.

Keno runners make a lot less than cocktail waitresses or dealers. They also work a lot harder, running all over the casino. But Preston wouldn't dream of dealing twenty-one or roulette, because "it's stationary, in one place, and you have someone over your back constantly. At least in keno you move around."

The tips can be small, though. "A lot of people don't think about toking when they win big because they're very excited and they usually forget," says Preston.

Sometimes you will have people who will come back later and tip, but usually they're so excited they collect their money and leave.

Once upon a time, tipping was very good and people were generous. These days you hardly ever get a person to tip you when they win. The majority of them, they'll give you a dollar or two, maybe $5 or $10, but very rarely do you have a customer who will be really nice and give you $100. Those days are long gone.

One of the casino trends of the 1980s is the video keno machine, but Hale of the Riviera insists the live game is more advantageous for the player. "If it does hit, you're going to win more on live keno," she says.

Plus you have the luxury of sitting and relaxing and watching the number being called rather than having this thing beeping at you. It's more personal. It's not like playing with a machine, you're actually playing the game with someone.

The odds may be bad on keno, but they do pay off occasionally—as in the 1987 instance of Los Angeles housewife Patte Gilbert. She started playing keno during a break one day from the blackjack tables and quickly won $1,500. "I guess I was just lucky—my numbers came up." Over the next twelve hours, she handed back to Bally's her big new bankroll in $5 and $10 keno tickets, along with poker and blackjack losses.

I go by that old saying—I'm playing with your money. It's a little fantasy. It's like playing with Monopoly money. Here you've got all this money, and it's fun to pretend.

Usually it gets so bad that, after you play keno for a while, you think, I can't even get up and have something to eat; my number will come up.

She won't play keno in the coffee shop because only even keno games are played there; she hates to miss the odd games. "God forbid your $1,500 game comes up and you're eating eggs and a bagel. It's just me against the keno balls. I am in control of my destiny."

ROULETTE

Some $74,100,000 was lost on the 154 roulette wheels in Clark County in 1987. House advantage: 5.26 percent, except for the "five-number bet" (0, 00, 1, 2, and 3), which yields a 5 percent advantage.

Spin the wheel and predict which number the ball will land on; or guess whether the number

Vegas roulette, 1950s style

will be red or black. Those are the two basic objects of roulette, Europe's most popular table game, but Vegas's least favorite. In Europe, roulette is played with only one 0; Americans play it with a 0 and a 00, which favors the house.

"In Europe, with just one zero, the house advantage is cut in half," says Munari.

"We tried playing it with just one zero, but that didn't do anything to help," says Jack Binion of the Horseshoe Club, which has just two roulette wheels. "Nobody wanted to play it, period. It just doesn't have the appeal that other games have."

But roulette can pay nicely, if you pick the right number. Put down $5 on the 5, have it come up, and your $5 will be worth $165. Put it on red, and you've got $10. Most players (or "rookies," as Bally's roulette dealer Joe Napoli calls them) will make a four-way bet, which places a chip on four numbers instead of one and dilutes the payoff to 7–1, instead of the heftier 35–1 for one number.

"I think they are playing for therapy more than anything else," says Napoli. "They want to hold on to their money longer and not have to worry about losing it. Most people that are serious about the game and want to make some money at it will play splits [two numbers] and straight-ups [one number]."

It is possible to make money at roulette, says Napoli, but only by playing for short periods of time.

It's not a game you're going to win a whole lot of money on, anyway. It's kind of like a hit-and-run proposition. You've got to get in and get out. The law of averages doesn't play in this game. You're betting against where a little ivory ball will fall.

As far as dealing the game, the trick of the trade is being able to move large piles of different-colored chips back and forth for eight hours a day and still remember which player belongs to what color. Says Riviera roulette dealer Tullio Marchionne:

Joe Napoli spins the roulette wheel at Bally's

You have to know what to watch for and be able to calculate the various different payoffs, which at times involve large quantities of chips or various conversions from smaller chips to larger-denomination chips. Some of it just comes naturally. You know how they say some ball players have a feel for their court, like in basketball? Well, here you've got to have the feel for the game.

To be any kind of a Vegas dealer requires being "a certain kind of person," says Marchionne.

You have to be prepared to put up with some verbal abuse. I've been called every name in the book. They've called me everything but Tullio. I've even been threatened physically. They've told me that they'd be waiting for me after I got off work. But I knew it was the whiskey talking, not them.

I try not to take it personally. Some people can lose $11,000 and give me a $500 tip, too. With roulette they can't really accuse me of anything. I just spin the ball. I can't even look at the wheel, and no one knows where it's going to land.

But as far as the money and the benefits go, Vegas casino dealing does have its up side. "It's been very good to me," says Napoli.

It just can get tedious and boring. The best part of the job is the people that you meet. You meet some very interesting people, and I don't mean just movie stars and athletes, I mean just everyday people from all over the world.

RACE AND SPORTS BETTING

Some $69,500,000 was lost in the thirty-two race and sports books in Clark County in 1987. House advantage: 18 percent for race bets; 4 percent for sports.

One of the newest trends in Vegas gambling over the past few years has been the introduction of the "race and sports book," a sports lounge within the casino where wagers are accepted on every type of game: football, basketball, baseball, hockey—you name it. Here gamblers are allowed to be creative in their bets. Want to predict who will play in and win the next Super Bowl? At the race and sports book, players can put money on their prognostications any time of the year.

Inside the race and sports books are giant television monitors showing various games from across the country. Gamblers can come in and watch free sports all day long, and get free coffee, beer, and hot dogs as they watch the games.

"Sports books are the fastest-growing segment of the gaming industry," says Frontier race and sports book manager Lenny del Genio. "They are growing around 200 percent a year."

The Frontier is one of the smaller books in town. Caesars and the Las Vegas Hilton go the super route: the Hilton's "super" book occupies 30,500 square feet, with forty-six video screens (many of which measure nine feet by twelve feet).

And business is booming. Credit the advent of cable TV and home satellite dishes, which give viewers the potential to watch anywhere from five to fifteen different games a day. Through more television, the public has become more interested in sports, particularly in Vegas. In just a few years, race and sports books have overtaken poker, bingo, and the big six wheels, to run just about even with roulette and keno. "It's the yuppie game," says del Genio.

We've grown up with computers and know-how to work databases. Anyone can become a handicapper and come up with a line on a sporting event with a database. The sports bettor is the most sophisticated in the world. They are the best-educated and some of the most well-rounded people I know. You have everybody playing, from attorneys and CPAs to guys that work in the car wash.

The only drawback to monster profits is the low commission the state allows sports books to make on the games: 2.5 percent. Until those numbers change, sports betting isn't likely to overtake craps and blackjack.

Because of the percentage, says del Genio, sports books can't take care of their good customers in the same way the casino can. No free rooms (although players qualify for a discounted room rate); an occasional hot dog and beer on the house is about it.

Sports bettor Lem Banker, a former New Jersey bookie, spends from $10,000 to $100,000 every day betting on sports games. "No cards, no horses, no tables, no machines," he says. "I only bet on human beings."

A day in the gambler's life: He awakes at nine-thirty, eats breakfast, works the telephone, and at twelve-thirty jumps in his Mercedes convertible to visit the casinos (Palace Station, Circus Circus, the Stardust, Riviera, Little Caesars, and Caesars Palace) to get a feel for their numbers—odds on the games—that day. "If their numbers are different from my numbers, I'll make a bet."

The afternoon will be spent at the casinos. He returns home at five, watches the news, and then works out with weights and in the pool for the next hour. He takes his wife out for dinner around eight, comes home, and watches the news and Johnny Carson's monologue. Then he really gets down to business. Banker sits up with his calculator and sports forms, preparing his odds for the games. "That way," he says, "when I get up, I'm ready."

"I'm not afraid to buck the trend," he says. "I can watch a baseball game and watch a pitcher throw a no-hitter, and I can't wait to bet on him four days later."

What he won't do is invest his winnings in the stock market.

Caesars is the scene of many championship bouts—and will gladly take your wagers on them.

109

The Olympiad Race and Sports
Book at Caesars Palace

I don't want any chairman of the board or somebody I don't know making decisions for me. When they bail out, they might tell a few close friends, and you're left holding the bag. I'd rather watch somebody drop a pass or a guy strike out or fumble a ball. I know his heart's in it, and I'll take my chances.

POKER

Some $56,100,000 was lost on the 531 poker tables of Clark County in 1987.
Says veteran poker ace Bobby Baldwin:

Poker is the only game in Las Vegas where you are competing against other players instead of the house. If you beat the twenty-one or craps table, you get just so much satisfaction. But if you beat Jack [Strauss] or Doyle [Brunson] or me—well, that's the greatest thing in the world.

Most casinos have poker rooms, where players are charged an hourly fee, or a 10 percent "rake" of the pot for using the tables. But beware: Poker players with little experience can get eaten alive by the poker pros at the tables, and the rakes on the small-limit tables will eat up profits.

To make some real bucks, the high-stakes poker game is the place to go, where potential big winnings clearly offset the rakes. High-stakes poker games are played daily in the poker rooms, but the biggest of them all is the annual twenty-one-day World Series of Poker tournament at Binion's Horseshoe Club every May.

The tournament began in 1949 when legendary gambler Nick "the Greek" Dandalos came to town looking for a no-limit, high-stakes poker game that he could play against one opponent. Benny Binion offered it to him. The game (against Dallas gambler Johnny Moss) lasted five months, with occasional breaks for sleep. Moss eventually won, and the Greek went home, so the story says, $2,000,000 in the hole.

In 1970, the Series became a regular event. It attracts three or four thousand poker players from all over the world—the biggest names (like Doyle Brunson, Puggy Pearson, and Bobby Baldwin) and the best Friday and Saturday hometown poker pros. They spend anywhere from $500 to $10,000 to buy in and play games that range from seven-card stud to Texas Hold-em, the traditional final game of the tourney. Potential winnings: anywhere from $300,000 to $700,000.

Poker face

"Some man lost a lot of money in Las Vegas. He's fed up, he's disgusted, he's driving out of town. From out of the mountains he hears a voice saying, 'Go back to Las Vegas, go back to Las Vegas.' He figures this is a good omen. He drives back to Las Vegas at eighty miles an hour. He gets back to Las Vegas; the voice says, 'Go into the Sands Hotel to gamble this time.' So he goes into the Sands Hotel. The voice says, 'Play roulette, put $2,000 on number eight.' He does that. Number six comes up. He loses. The voice says, 'How about that?'"

—Henny Youngman

THE BIG SIX

Some $7,700,000 was lost on the forty-one big six wheels of Clark County in 1987. House advantage: 20 percent.

Besides roulette, the other wheel of the casino is the "big six," also known as the "Wheel of Fortune." It is the casino equivalent of the carnival Skillo wheel, strictly try-your-luck time, as players put down $1, $2, $5, $10, $20, or $100 and predict where the wheel will stop. Most times it has a habit of not stopping where people think it will. It is not a good investment, but it sure is simple.

"A lot of the people who play the slots play the big six wheel because it's easy," says Riviera big six dealer Kathy Hagan. "Sometimes they just want to get away from the twenty-one or craps tables. Everyone will come over here sooner or later for something to do."

"A terrible place to bet," says Munari, "strictly a sucker's bet." With a house advantage of 20 percent, every time the wheel is spun and $1 is bet, 20 percent is given right over to the casino.

Big six dealers, like poker-room managers but unlike other game dealers, call out in the casino and urge players to stop by and try their luck at the Wheel of Fortune.

"To deal big six is no big deal," says Bill Bischoff of Caesars Palace. "You just have to make sure the wheel turns a minimum of four times—and be a barker. You've got to promote that one."

"It's a very social game," says Hagan. "It's more social than the other games. They can get pretty serious on those games when they make $25 bets."

"Dealing the big six is all about talking to people, carnival-style," says Joey Maxim, a former boxer who deals big six at the Frontier. "A lot of the older people still know me, and older people are the ones that gamble. I would never do the other games. I don't think I could handle them. With big six I can move back and forth and take pictures with people."

Former boxer Joey Maxim, a Frontier Big Six dealer

Big Six dealer Kathy Thorpe from the Riviera

112

Bingo at Sam's Town

BINGO

The eighteen bingo rooms of Clark County lost $1,500,000 in 1987.

Vegas-style bingo looks nothing like Thursday evening at the church. It's a high-pressure, high-stakes, super-fast game; players tend to have eight to twelve cards in front of them per game. Some women have been known to play with as many as twenty-one bingo cards, their hands moving at breakneck speed to fill them up.

The payoffs aren't too bad in Vegas bingo—some hotels pay three to five hundred dollars for a winning card, not too shabby for an investment of anywhere from a quarter to $4 a card. For all the high pressure of the games, the bingo rooms are different from the poker or baccarat areas in that they have a clientele of regulars who all get to know each other. A bingo caller in Vegas has a relationship with the player similar to that of a coffee-shop waitress with the morning crowd.

"Bingo is the best job in town for a woman," says Bea DeSanto, who works the Palace Station bingo room, calling games, selling cards, and making payoffs. "Everybody comes in happy; nobody gets angry if they lose, like they would at the dice table. We actually take very little abuse from the customers."

The Palace Station was originally called the "Bingo Palace" when it opened. It has long been known as one of the busiest bingo houses in Vegas, along with Sam's Town, the Showboat, and the Holiday Casino. But even with five sessions a day and a packed house, DeSanto says bingo makes no money. "It's a draw," she says. "It brings the people in. . . . They leave here after the sessions and play the slots."

DeSanto has the fun task of pulling bingo balls out of the bowl and issuing bingo-isms like "B-9, that's B-9" and "I-37 . . . that's I-37" over the microphone. That's her favorite part of the job. "I love seeing the expression on their face when you call their number," says DeSanto, who adds that her all-time favorite bingo number is B-6. "I don't know why this is, but it's the number I tend to call a lot," she says. "There are certain numbers all of us girls call. With Carol it's B-6. Dolores is O-24. Everybody claps when I read B-6."

TWO MEN YOU WANT TO GET TO KNOW AT THE CASINO

The Casino Manager

The floorman watches the dealer. The pit boss watches the floorman. The shift boss watches the pit boss. But the entire house is watched by the casino manager.

He is the most important individual within the gambling establishment. The hotel president keeps track of the entire picture, but the casino manager is in charge of everything that happens in the casino—the tables, the slots, the dealers, the race and sports books, the poker rooms—everything related to gambling. His job is to get people to spend money. He's happy when that is accomplished. Feeling bad watching people lose isn't part of the job: "It's his money. He can do whatever he chooses to do with it," says Sahara casino manager John Boni.

If a guy comes in with $100,000 or $200,000 and wants to play, hey, listen, God bless 'im. You know, he could beat us for $100,000 or $200,000 also. If he wins, I have to pay him, so I can't feel too sorry for him if he loses, because it works both ways. He's not going to feel sorry for me if I have to pay him $100,000. We're businesspeople, and we're here to win. It's our business. This is our business. This isn't just some fun thing that we only do on Friday and Saturday nights.

So, in other words, the casino manager *wants* the players to lose?

"Absolutely," Boni says. "It's not that I'm rooting for them to lose, but, naturally, if it works out that way it's to my benefit. But while they're here, you can rest assured that they will have a good time."

Sahara casino manager John Boni with Redd Foxx, members of the Bon Jovi rock group, and an unidentified friend.

In the 1985 film *Lost in America*, the character played by Albert Brooks has a downright terrible time losing money in Vegas. He awakens one morning to discover—in horror—that his wife has blown $100,000 at the roulette wheel while he was slumbering. He begs the casino manager to give the money back as a grand public relations gesture. Guess how the casino manager responds.

No one has ever come right out and played that scene in front of Boni, but they have begged for other considerations after depleting their bankrolls.

What they will ask for? Nine out of ten times, it is airfare to get back home. We will provide round-trip airfare, and there are occasions where I will allocate some pocket money. I will allocate $1,000 or so just for the guy to have some walking-around money. And I will tell them in a very nice fashion, "Don't play it; just keep it in your pocket."

Fast-talking John Boni is a former garment industry executive from New York City. He met his wife, Vegas entertainer Sue Kim, in the Big Apple. They married there and gave the city a try, but her heart remained on the Strip (where she has a successful act at the Holiday casino with her two brothers). After a year in New York, they moved to Vegas, where they share a home with a teenage boy and girl and twenty musical instruments (ranging from bagpipe to piano, guitar, sax, and vibes, all of which Kim plays onstage).

Boni works from ten-thirty to four in the afternoon, comes home for dinner, and returns to the casino at eight, where he stays till around one. Kim goes to the show room at seven and leaves around one-thirty. They both work six nights a week. The casino manager says he would like to spend more time at home,

but it's the nature of the business. We're open twenty-four hours a day, it's very very hard just to work one shift and be successful in this type of operation. You have to touch base with all your people.

I am a marriage counselor, I am a psychiatrist, a priest, rabbi, you name it. I spend very few hours in the office. I'm not an office person. I spend my evenings constantly walking around in all areas of the casino watching what's going on, making sure everything is going smoothly, dealers are working properly, nobody's fooling around, customers are not being abused, and looking out for cheats.

You don't mind losing, but you want to make sure you're getting a straight count, and by that I mean that nobody's cheating you. In today's market, it will sound James Bondish to people who really don't know about gaming, but they've got all kinds of computers and calculators and ways to cheat us, and as soon as we come up with more ways to deter it, they come up with more ways to counteract it. So it's a constant, ongoing situation. We never let our guard down. We are always on the lookout for suspects.

And what happens then—does the Sahara beat them up? "Nah, those days are long gone," he says.

We tell him, "We don't want your play; take it down the street. Don't come back here." Once they know we're on to them, ninety-nine out of a hundred times they will back away gracefully, take their winnings, and leave. Sometimes they yell back and claim they're not cheating. If they're not house customers and not staying in the hotel, we ask them to come back another day and tell them we won't try to press any charges. If they're staying here, we'll give them a complimentary stay and say try your luck next time.
We're all watching [for cheaters]; it's our business. The cash and the chips are our inventory. That's our product. Our commodity is cash. We keep track of it. Everybody says, "Why is that guy watching me so seriously?" He's watching the money in the rack, plus or minus. Because, after that eight-hour period, for the games that he has been responsible for, he has to come up with a general figure as to where he stands for the evening, and that's how we get our inventory.

Besides watching over the cash and chips, the casino manager is also in charge of the markers. He makes the major decisions on whether or not to issue credit. The pit boss is allowed to approve anything up to $20,000, but the casino manager takes over after that. Most players don't like to come to town with big sums in their pockets; they prefer to play on credit and pay their bill when they get home.

If you as a player were to stumble in here in the middle of the night and were looking for $100,000 or $150,000, whatever the figure may be, I would have to okay it. If I'm not here, somebody's going to have to call me at home. When we get our Friday-night millionaires coming in here and saying, "Don't you know me?" you've got to be prepared to make the decision. After a couple of years, you can develop a sixth sense about them—you'll know whether you're making the right decision or not. Sometimes you win, sometimes you lose, but most of the time I'm right.
Most of the time I can tell by looking at somebody and hearing their conversation whether there are A) good for the money, or B) just giving me a song-and-dance routine.

For many years the marker was a debt of honor, not a legally enforceable debt. Nowadays, the casinos can sue a player if he doesn't pay up. But collecting from a gambler is nevertheless a very delicate proposition.

The most important thing is, while you don't want to lose

Sahara casino manager John Boni with Sugar Ray Leonard

the money, you also don't want to lose the customer, because if you do lose the customer, he's only going to go down the street and play. So I may say to a guy, "Okay, you owe me $10,000. If you want to come in with cash, put a couple thousand towards your back balance and play with whatever you have in your pocket." It pacifies him; it gives him a shot to try and win his money back. I don't lose a customer, and I get a chance at the fresh cash he has.

Boni started in Vegas as a manager of the Golden Nugget's baccarat room, advancing to pit floorman there and at the Tropicana, before moving on to shift manager (the job above pit boss and below casino manager) at the Trop and the Fremont. He has run the casino at the Stardust, Fremont, Marina, and Hacienda hotels, as well as at the Sahara. Today, all of these are basically middle-market "grind" joints, but he says that when he first got to town, things used to be quite different.

It was a different era. We had the only game in town; there was no Atlantic City. We had a lot of heavy high rollers; now we're dealing with Mr. and Mrs. America, who make small bets. In that era, the high roller came to Las Vegas more frequently. Now we've got 60,000 rooms available here. Ten to fifteen years ago we had a handful of places; you had to actually know somebody in a casino in Las Vegas to get a room.

A man you want to get to know: longtime Frontier casino host Mort ("Mr. Frontier") Saiger

The Host

In the old days they were called "greeters," up-front guys like Jakie Freedman at the Sands and the Desert Inn's Wilbur Clark, who took care of the customers and said hello. Today, the greeter has evolved into the "host." Vegas's first: Mort Saiger, "Mr. Frontier."

A former Los Angeles milk-truck driver, Saiger began his gaming career at the Last Frontier as a jack-of-all-trades, a job that eventually evolved into twenty-one dealing. He left in 1952 and moved around to various casinos, before returning to the Frontier in 1969. His new job was to watch over the blackjack tables, but Saiger found that he spent more of his time on the telephone, dealing with clients he had developed a relationship with over the years. The bosses told Saiger to forget about twenty-one— just take care of his customers, looking after them as the "host" of the casino.

"The cards, the dice, the tables, they're the same all over," says Saiger. "It's that human touch that makes the difference. When they come in, greet them, pay attention to them, and don't make them feel like a stranger. That is the duty of the host."

Hosts like Saiger roam the floor of the casino, watching for the players spending time at the tables, dropping big money on the games. They walk up and introduce themselves.

We ask him how he got here, whether he came on his own, and if there is anything we can do to make his stay more pleasant. From then on, he feels he has been welcomed by somebody. Next time he wants reservations, instead of calling a travel agent, he calls me.

Most hosts are former pit bosses; many also come from the world of professional sports, with ex-boxers, rodeo riders, and baseball players predominating. Virtually every major casino now has a team of hosts who are assigned to take care of individual gamblers.

Gene Kilroy, Muhammad Ali's former business manager, came to Vegas after Ali's boxing career ended. The hotels were eager to tap into his vast array of contacts in the entertainment, business, and sports worlds.

In my industry, I've had calls from customers who wanted to see a heart specialist in Houston [get] fight tickets, [arrange for] flights, baseball games, football games, Broadway shows. To be a good host you must reach out to all avenues in life. If a guy is a stockbroker and his client calls and says, "I need tickets to a Broadway show," and he says, "I can't get them," he's going to look for somebody who can. This is my key to the success of my business. Everybody needs somebody, and I need friends. In this business, when you have a friend and don't abuse a friend, they'll come back.

No matter who you are, no matter where you travel, no matter where you go, if you go into a city and don't know anybody, it's a lonely city. But once you know somebody. . . . I defy someone to leave this hotel and tell me they didn't enjoy themselves. A guy could come here and lose $1,000,000, but he'll say "I was treated well." A woman can come in and lose $1,000 in a slot machine, but she'll say the people are nice, the rooms are great, the food was outstanding.

Hosts spend their nights patroling the casino floors and their days working the phones, calling their list of gamblers. "We tell them we miss them," says Saiger. "We ask them if everything is all right. We keep in touch. We want them to know that somebody's thinking of them." Hosts can take cold phone calls as well from gamblers who have heard about their hotels and want to come for a visit. "I'll find out who they are," says Kilroy.

If he is a $5,000,000 player, I'll say I'm going to send our airplane to pick you up, because you could either win $5,000,000 or lose $5,000,000. If he calls and says he's a friend of Joe Brown's and is a $5,000 player, I'll say we'll set up a $5,000 line of credit. If he plays up to it, we'll take care of his room, food, and beverage.

Saiger's clientele is all stored in a big computer, as well as the traditional little black book. That part of the new technology he likes. He's not, however, a fan of the tracking system developed to qualify players for comps. "It was a different atmosphere in the old days," he says. "They weren't so strict with picking up a man's room or giving him this or that. Now, with computers, you have to justify every reason why you comp this man."

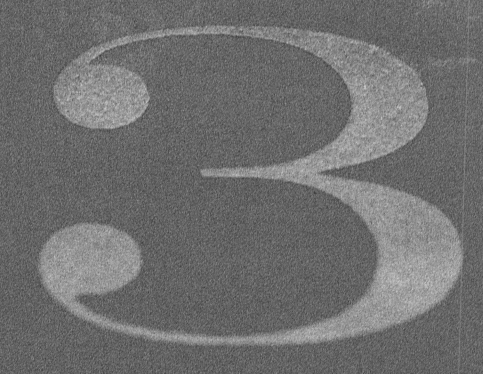

PART THREE

3

THAT'S ENTERTAINMENT

CHAPTER 7
Stars of the Strip

"Do we have anyone in love tonight?" asks the singer. "Do we have anyone in love just for the night? We do? Excuse me sir, is this your wife or are you on a business trip?"

Laughter.

You got married four hours ago? What the hell are you doing here? I'm going to do a song for our newlyweds. It's going to be a song we hadn't planned on doing, but that hasn't stopped us yet this evening. Captain, would you please bring this couple a bottle of champagne on me? You know, the Indian all dressed up like a wedding cake. See the guy who hasn't been applauding for the whole show? Bill it to him.

More yucks.

The singer proceeds to croon "You Don't Have to Say You Love Me" for the couple, and then walks off the stage. The audience stands, claps, and hollers.

The entertainer comes back.

"You keep that up, we'll be here another twenty minutes."

More applause.

"How about another hour?"

Even more applause.

"Oh, what the hell . . . how 'bout another hour and a half?"

The applause is really wild now.

Wayne Newton: "Ladies and gentlemen, you've been a very special audience."

Wayne ("The Midnight Idol") Newton backstage in his dressing room

"If you really want to break the casino, let's go for broke and keep the show going for three hours."

At this point the audience is crazy.

You know, ladies and gentlemen, we don't often get a crowd like you . . . this early. But seriously, folks, you're such a very special audience that we're going to attempt a song now that we save for very special occasions, of which this is one. This is our special song . . . I hope you like it.

The tom-toms start to beat, the lasers are lit, the smoke of the dry ice machine rolls out into the audience, and the singer begins to speak the opening lines of a quintessential Vegas show-room tune: "Spring was never waiting for us, dear . . . "

The point of this story is to illustrate that *the* singer of "MacArthur Park," Wayne Newton, *the* King of the Strip, is also *the* hardest-working man in show business. He changes his clothes at least once during every show (the giant belt buckle with the big eagle comes on in the second half). He sings, he tells jokes, he plays the guitar, banjo, piano, and violin; he kisses the ladies in the front row. Other performers play an hour; Newton does two.

The hardest-working man in show business is also known as Mr. Las Vegas Show Business—

Al Jolson, Elvis Presley, and Sammy Davis, Jr., all rolled into one. But what exactly is Las Vegas Show Business? Let's ask Mr. Jerry Lewis: It's all about "seeing a performer sweat. If you do what you're supposed to do and sweat, then you'll be really successful in Vegas."

Perspiration, per Lewis. Schmaltz and glitz, according to others. "Do you know the definition of the word *glitz*?" asks Sammy Davis, Jr.

What is it? . . . I love when they say, "And they brought their normal Las Vegas—type show in." What do they mean? Las Vegas is the Mecca of nightclub show business, so, to me, if you bring in a Vegas nightclub show, you bring in the very best. What are you going to bring in? A typical Cleveland-type show?

Sammy Davis, Jr., has been playing Vegas since 1945. Dean Martin, Frank Sinatra, and Don Rickles since the 1950s. Newton, Tom Jones, Engelbert Humperdinck, and Cosby since the 1960s. Vegas is an incredibly loyal town. Once you become a star—and prove that gamblers will come to watch you over and over—chances are you can fill those show rooms for years.

"Playing Vegas can give an act broader appeal throughout the world," says Caesars entertainment director Allan Bregman.

They're not always going to have a number-one hit record, but they can build and develop a following here. They can also sustain it for the next twenty to twenty-five years and still play Vegas. They still have a place to work. If they had taken the position that Vegas was beneath them many years ago, after the record died out, that would have been the end of them.

"Is this an audience or an oil painting?"

—Milton Berle

Sammy and Jerry, show room pals since the reign of the "Old Vegas" in the 1950s, backstage at Bally's in 1987

An invariable episode in Engelbert
Humperdinck's act

Indeed, a lot of performers won't play Vegas because it just ain't hip to play there. Ron Wood of the Rolling Stones was asked once if he could ever envision the Stones playing Vegas. He said he'd rather be dead.

"The new stars that come up just aren't hungry," says Davis. "They get a record, they do one show at a stadium for $80,000, and leave. Who wants to work a week at some crummy hotel for $400,000? They make that in three days. That's the mentality."

Vegas execs question whether the hot new young acts would draw the audiences anyway. "Las Vegas tends to draw an older crowd, because the people that gamble are older," says veteran Vegas producer Maynard Sloate. "As the younger people learn to gamble, Las Vegas will start appealing to them."

Bregman says he regularly has calls in to Billy Joel, Neil Diamond, and Elton John asking them to play Vegas. But he always gets turned down. So he goes back to the drawing board and ends up with a lot of the same acts. Nevertheless, he continues to search for new blood.

"You have to find attractions that are not hard rock, that have had a young contemporary following, and have grown over the years," he says, adding that what works today is not necessarily what worked in 1980.

A lot of the older names that have played there over the years, their fans and their audience are beginning to die out. The audience has changed. The age level of people that are going to Vegas, it's a much wider audience than it used to be.

For years bookers felt a young contemporary performer just wouldn't cut it, that the gamblers wouldn't come see them. Bernie Rothkopf, then president of the MGM Grand Hotel, told an interviewer in 1980 that Bob Dylan or the Rolling Stones would bomb in a Vegas show room. "There are a lot of recording artists who sell millions of records but who can't relate to the Las Vegas audience," he said. "It's more than just voice and presentation. You have to be a complete entertainer to perform here. You can't just stand up and play."

"One is listening and the other is watching," says Wayne Newton. "If they wanted to see the record, they'd stay home and listen."

There are exceptions, but virtually every modern performance by a Vegas superstar will follow at least one of these rules:

- Rule One: It could be beginning, middle, or end, but at some point in the show the dry ice machine will begin to fill the stage with smoke.
- Rule Two: The lights will be lowered and the spotlight will focus on the mirrored ball on the ceiling, which will then begin to revolve.
- Rule Three: The singer will croon his tune surrounded by a rain curtain, giving the effect of a wet serenader onstage (he's actually as dry as the folks out front).
- Rule Four: Someone in the audience is going to have to participate. That could be in the form of a kiss from Wayne, a handshake from Siegfried or Roy—or Engelbert Humperdinck pulling a pretty woman onstage so he can sing to her and get her to put her hands in his shirt.

Cugie and Charo

The first question tourists usually ask when they get off the airplane and into a cab is "Who's in town?"

The second is "Who's the highest paid?"

That's easy. Sinatra's numero uno, at $525,000 a week, closely followed by Cosby at $500,000 (or $100,000 a night). Newton is good for $400,000 a week. Siegfried and Roy, who work more often than anyone else, split $11,500,000 a year.

Your basic top ten Vegas "superstars" of the 1980s would be Sinatra, Cosby, Newton, Engelbert, Tom Jones, Sammy, Dean, Siegfried and Roy, Diana Ross, and Julio Iglesias. The days of the sexy female song-and-dance act—like Ann-Margret and Juliet Prowse—seem to be history. Suzanne Somers and Charo have been playing the smaller clubs, but they don't attract the crowds like they used to.

The salary wars began with the opening of the Riviera in 1955, when Liberace was paid $50,000 a week to open the joint, which was at the time a record sum for anybody. The Riviera topped itself in the 1980s when it paid Dolly Parton $300,000 a week. The Hilton and Bally's joined the half a million era in 1986 and 1987 with their big checks for Cosby and Sinatra, respectively. The record salaries delight performer and agent, but there will always be critics arguing that no one entertainer is worth that much change.

"The stars always take a bashing when it comes to dollars," says Bill Cosby.

But you know, I'm in this business to make money. General Motors makes cars, Boeing builds airplanes—you can't walk in and get a freebie. You can get a rebate if you're not selling, but I'm in it to make money. Now if I walk in and charge a guy $75,000

Bill Cosby doing his act in Vegas, mid-1960s

a week, and he decides that I'm a major star and he's going to charge people $40 a ticket and give 'em two drinks and a bowl of peanuts and the room holds 1,500 people, and I do two shows a night—what does that come out to?

It comes to $720,000 for six nights of performances.

On top of that, if the people are excited about seeing me, and the hotel is full, I get no percentage of room service, I get no percentage of liquor sales, I get no percentage from the valet parking guys, no percentage of the restaurants, which are overflowing, and I certainly don't get a kickback from the casino. So when they say nobody's worth that, it's possible for the proper headliner to go into a room like the Hilton's—and that guy or woman could charge $600,000 a week—and the hotel would make a tremendous profit.

Vegas performers used to come out of vaudeville and the nightclub circuit. Today, they come out of television, the comedy clubs, and the international entertainment circuit. Mary Hart was able to parlay her TV exposure on "Entertainment Tonight" into a ready audience when she made her Vegas debut in 1988. Iglesias is able to draw on his large base of international—and American—fans for his regular shows at Caesars' Circus Maximus.

"Julio is one of the rare exceptions that recognized that if he can develop himself as an entertainer and not worry about having a record all the time, that he's going to have a long life playing the casinos, and has developed quite a following," says Bregman. Caesars bet well when they hired Iglesias, because he turned out to be one of its best draws. His Latin good looks and sexy voice attract the wives of the high rollers, who sit together in the show room while their husbands gamble in the casino. The casino regularly turns away five hundred women a night—at $45 a head—when he plays. He can play Vegas forever.

But not everybody can pull it off. Carroll O'Connor, Demond Wilson, Telly Savalas, Wally Cox, McLean Stevenson, Sally Struthers, and Ted Knight all tried unsuccessfully to put together Vegas acts. Knight's was such a bomb he was asked to leave after the first show.

OPPOSITE:
Julio Iglesias likes the Vegas lights.

Mary Hart of TV's "Entertainment Tonight" had a dream all her life—to play Vegas. Here she is in her flower-filled suite at the Golden Nugget the morning after her April 1988 opening.

127

Ann-Margret: she debuted in Las Vegas in 1960 and went on to star with Elvis Presley in 1963's *Viva Las Vegas.*

In the 1970s, Ann-Margret was known as the "Queen of the Strip," her energetic song-and-dance act paving the way for other women entertainers like Cher, Diana Ross, Lola Falana, Suzanne Somers, and Charo. Cher, Charo, and Lola rarely play Vegas anymore, and Ann-Margret took a breather herself from 1983 to 1988. But Ann-Margret— who was discovered by George Burns at the Dunes in 1960, just before she went on to movies like *Bye, Bye Birdie, Carnal Knowledge,* and *Viva Las Vegas*—signed a rich five-year contract with Caesars to return to the Strip. Her opening in November 1988 was an attempt to return to the tradition of the female Vegas headliner.

But because there are so few new Vegas superstars coming up in the ranks, male or female, Wayne Newton sees his breed as an endangered species. Once he and Sammy and Engelbert and the others hang up their hats, Las Vegas Show Business is going to have a rather dry spell.

"There were two guys who I thought could have picked up the torch and carried on our tradition," he says. "One was Donny [Osmond], because he spent his entire life in this industry and is extremely talented, and the other is Michael [Jackson], who, as we all know, went on to carve his own niche in this industry."

ANN-MARGRET

Of all the stars who have played Vegas, only two have hotel suites named after them. Not Frank Sinatra, Sammy Davis, Jr., Wayne Newton, Siegfried and Roy. Not Cher. Just two co-stars of the 1964 movie *Viva Las Vegas:* Elvis Presley—at the Las Vegas Hilton—and Ann-Margret, at Caesars.

In 1960 an eighteen-year-old Swede from Chicago—former member of the Suttletones—made her Vegas debut in the Dunes lounge. At the end of the engagement, Ann-Margret went to Los Angeles, where she auditioned for George Burns, who was preparing an act for the Sahara Hotel.

"She said, 'I can sing as well as Bobby Darin,' " recalls Burns. " 'I also move as well as he does.' She sang two songs for me, and by the time she got to the end of the second number, she moved so well she had dusted off all the furniture."

Burns hired her on the spot. In the Sahara's Conga Room, she sang "Bill Bailey" and "Mack the Knife" and did a duet and soft-shoe routine with the comedian. In the audience for the two-week gig were talent scouts from 20th Century-Fox and RCA Records, both of whom signed her up. In February 1961 her first album, *And Here She Is! Ann-Margret* was released, complete with liner notes from Burns. Her first film, *A Pocketful of Miracles,* directed by Frank Capra, opened in the spring. Rodgers and Hammerstein's *State Fair* debuted late that summer, with her playing opposite Pat Boone. Then came the movies *Bye, Bye Birdie* and *Viva Las Vegas.* In the latter, she played a hotel swimming instructor who falls in love with race-car driver Presley. "It's that go-go guy and that bye-bye gal in the fun capital of the world," blared the movie-poster blurb.

Ann-Margret started headlining in Vegas in 1967 at the Riviera, with a show that established *the* Vegas energetic female song-and-dance act. Her opening production number featured her and twelve guys on motorcycles. She closed the show with a tribute to a fictional gal named Mimi, a go-go girl who invents a short skirt for dancing. And she sang "Satisfaction." It was this act that other female performers like Lola Falana, Suzanne Somers, Charo, Lynda Carter, and Mary Hart used as a model in the 1970s and '80s.

In 1972 Ann-Margret fell twenty-two feet from a prop on a Lake Tahoe stage and had to undergo reconstructive mouth surgery. Five months later she was riding a motorcycle again on the stage of the Las Vegas Hilton.

She puts forth so much energy onstage that she has little time for sunlight in Vegas. "The adrenalin is so high that I usually get to bed at seven in the morning, sleep until four [P.M.], have breakfast, do some exercises, and then go do the show. What's difficult is when I come back home. For four days I AM UP. I cannot go to sleep."

Ann-Margret stopped playing Vegas in 1983 to care for her husband, Roger Smith, who suffers from a rare form of muscular dystrophy. By 1988, she was ready to return to the show room. Caesars signed her to a two-year deal to play ten weeks a year in Vegas, Tahoe, and Atlantic City.

"I really missed the stage. Five years was such a long time. Do you realize just how long five years is? I'm just thrilled to be back up on that stage, because that's what I am, a live performer."

Says Burns: "I'm glad she went back. A lot of actresses can act, but what actress can play Vegas? Why should she give that up?"

And a word on her namesake Caesars Suite. Located in the Olympic Tower, it features a large jacuzzi with a view of the Strip. Other furnishings include a round bed, mirrored ceiling, and a round wet bar. You can check in for $860 a night.

THE LOUNGE

Talk to any performer about the good old days of Vegas, and the word *lounge* is sure to come up. That wonderful place where Shecky Greene, Louis Prima and Keely Smith, Wayne Newton, the Mary Kaye Trio, and Don Rickles would wow gamblers between show-room shows. They would perform till five in the morning. The lounges were "covered"—separate little show rooms where there was no admission; all you had to do was buy some drinks.

Young Wayne Newton got his first major job in Vegas in 1959, working with brother Jerry in the Fremont's Carnival Lounge. Greene, Rickles. Sam Butera, Louis and Keely, and Pete Barbutti

Shecky Greene

all became Vegas legends in the lounges. Acts could work the rooms for years, hoping eventually to get a booking in a larger venue.

"When they closed the lounges, they also closed the proving ground for the next step into the main room," says Davis.

The lounge was the proving ground for testing material, drawing people in, getting the customers used to you. And then, hey, when you got a chance, you went into that main room; that was a step. You went into the main room as the bottom half of the bill, but, hey, you made it into the main room. The next time you came back you might be headlining.

Shecky Greene started playing the lounges at a time when they were strictly for music only. He convinced the hotel bosses to let him do his act in the lounge when, after a week in the main room, he was told that there was no further work available for him. "I was very determined at the time," he says. "I was living in Beverly Hills, and I had all kinds of expenses, so I said to them, let me work the lounge. Playing the main room as the opening act wasn't satisfying to me. I was used to playing small rooms."

Greene had a contract with the Riviera, but they just didn't have an opening for him. "So when they said no, I said, 'You owe me; you'll either have to pay me or play me.' So they put me in the lounge. In the beginning it was kind of rough. I did four shows a night, seven nights a week. But then it took off."

All the Vegas stars would stop by after their shows to catch Greene, whose brand of comedy had achieved legendary status over the years. Rickles is known as the master of the insult, but Greene is a master of the off the cuff—audiences never knew what to expect: like the night drunk Sheck beat up three cops onstage who tried to restrain him; he won.

"In the lounge I created something," says Greene.

There wasn't the same kind of pressure as playing the main room. I could do anything I wanted to out in the lounge. Whatever happened to me, I would get right up on that stage and tell a joke. I would talk about getting divorced, or the fact that I had been arrested the night before. The audience loved to be let in on little things. They'd yell out, "Hey, did you get arrested today?"

A vintage Greene jail story:

I got arrested for being drunk last night. They threw me in a cell with a vicious murderer, and it was the first time I realized the judicial system in this country stinks. Because a half hour later the murderer was out and I was still in jail. So I yelled to the cops, "What's the matter, the murderer's free, what about me?" They said, "You're a drunk." I said, "Let me out, I'll murder someone."

In the lounge, a comedian could do comedy off the top of his head and go on as long as he wanted. In the main show room, the rule was ironclad—no show could last longer than an hour and ten minutes. The comedian who played the show generally had to stick to the time—or risk abuse from the casino boss, who wanted the audience back in his room gambling.

"When they said they wanted no more than an hour and ten minutes for the show, they meant it," says Milton Berle. "You had to get them out so they could gamble. I used to say when I closed my show, 'Thank you very much, ladies and gentlemen, you've been a wonderful audience; and, by the way—they're waiting for you out there.'"

The lounge era ended in the 1970s, as most of the lounge stars were getting booked in the main show rooms and folks started going to sleep earlier. "The town started to change," says Greene. "It was not the all-night town anymore, where people stayed up until four in the morning, sat in the lounge, and enjoyed themselves."

"I lost $36,000 in the coffee shop this morning waiting for a bagel. I was playing keno."

—Shecky Greene

131

Today, the lounge is no longer covered. It is an open area where Top 40 bands play and young couples dance to the hits—like any other dance club in America, only slicker.

"I don't mean this as a put-down to the kids who work here now, but it's a different type of performer who works in the open-air lounge," says Davis.

> These are good people, good musicians, but they're wasted. If my attitude to you is one of uncomfortability, and I don't really give a shit about our spending time together, I'm going to say, well, what the fuck am I doing here? It becomes contagious. The performer sees himself in an open-air arena, nobody's paying attention to him, so don't tell me I'm going to sing my heart out for you, because I can't.
>
> I can sing "Birth of the Blues" and "Mr. Bojangles" until I'm blue in the face, but I can't fight a cat wanting to hump a chick.
>
> They get good musicians who want the job, but in their heart of hearts they know that nobody's paying attention to them. And it becomes a 360-degree wow, man, I'm not going to disturb you too much, and you're not going to disturb me too much. That's the sad part. When the lounges were enclosed, there were two nightclubs in the same place—one place was just more informal than the other. That *was* Vegas.

Part of the fondness Davis feels for the lounge era extends to anything from the old days of Vegas. It's summed up in a word you'll hear from any entertainer who played back then: *camaraderie*. We're all in this together: performing together onstage. Hanging out after the show. Going to watch fellow performers in the lounge between shows. When Davis teamed with Jerry Lewis as an act at Bally's in 1987, Davis said he viewed the partnership as a "last hurrah for a certain kind of show business."

> What I meant was that, in the old days, if Danny Thomas was playing the Sands and Frank was in town, he'd go onstage, too. The Sands became the place—you don't know when Frank or Sammy is going to walk on the stage—but you knew that they might.

Davis has called Vegas his "spiritual home," a place that was tailor-made for his kind of life-style.

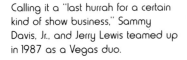

Calling it a "last hurrah for a certain kind of show business," Sammy Davis, Jr., and Jerry Lewis teamed up in 1987 as a Vegas duo.

It is the only city in the world that turns people on. People that you can look at and know exactly what their lives are—no matter what city—it's 10:45 in bed, news at 11, and maybe the first fifteen minutes of Johnny Carson. But then it's definitely sleepy-poo. But not here. When they come to Vegas, there must be something in the air—as soon as they get off the plane, it's instant swinger.

After all these years, Swingin' Sammy is still turning on Vegas audiences—not a bad feat for a performer who's been playing the town continually since 1945. At an average salary of $200,000 a week, it's easy to see why he still plays there. Money's great, surroundings comfortable, and he still enjoys "singing my heart out."

And they *do* treat him royally. In his "Ziegfeld Suite" at Bally's, a VCR and videodisc player have been hooked up to a giant-screen TV for him, along with a stereo system including a CD player. Davis brings up his substantial audio/video collection and watches movies in his room. He also cooks all of his meals up there.

When Tom Jones plays Vegas, he sleeps in his room all day until five—with the humidifier on—wakes up, and works out for two hours, sees people at seven, and then goes on stage at eight. Caesars switchboard operators are told never to put calls through to entertainers until after twelve noon.

Bill Cosby is different. When he plays Vegas, he's up at ten A.M. every morning and on the track by eleven. His entire afternoon is spent at the University of Nevada, running, working out, and getting away from the telephones. Cosby is the man *Forbes* magazine has called the richest in show business. So why, after all these years and all those millions, does he need to fly out from New York to do a week in Vegas?

"I don't have to play here," he says.

I do it because the people at the entertainment end of this hotel business generally understand what this business is all about. Las Vegas still represents good entertainment, a place for people to come and be naughty, and the naughtiness is a lot cleaner than it used to be. It is really conceivable that these show rooms could be shut down, because the stadiums now hold the major stars. I want to help keep the show rooms open.

When in Vegas, Cosby works out during the day at the running track.

THE TEN GREATEST SONGS OF THE VEGAS MAIN ROOMS

1. "The Way We Were"
2. "The Birth of the Blues"
3. "MacArthur Park"
4. "Feelings"
5. "New York, New York"
6. "America the Beautiful"
7. "The Battle Hymn of the Republic"
8. "Viva Las Vegas"
9. "C. C. Rider"
10. "Chicago"

MILTON BERLE IN VEGAS

Milton Berle started playing Vegas in 1952, at the Sands Hotel. He was "Mr. Television," at the height of his popularity heading up the top-rated "Texaco Star Theater." A veteran vaudeville performer, he was TV's first superstar, and the Sands' hiring him to headline the Copa Room for $37,500 a week back then was like getting Michael Jackson or Bruce Springsteen to play Caesars today.

"There must be people out there—
I hear breathing."

—Milton Berle

133

Berle was one of the first comics to introduce the Vegas gambling joke, a classic born of the Vegas boom in the 1950s. "I coined the phrase 'Lost Wages.' What a great play on words," Berle says.

"A waiter walks into the crowd with a stack of plates and I say, 'Who ordered another stack of chips?'

"'Did you win tonight, sir? You didn't? Oh, you're in the right place.'

"Anything that related to them. Anything that related to gambling they loved. ' . . . and then I was at the Circus Circus . . . losing, losing.'

"I'd go out and tummel. I wouldn't know what I was going to say. We had such looseness. We weren't the way they are today, with the four-letter words and everything. It was double entendre and risqué, but it wasn't filth. Today, they say *fuck* like *hello*. We never did that."

Milton Berle dealing twenty-one

The basic act: Berle welcomes everyone to the show, tells some jokes, and introduces the Amin Brothers, who do an acrobatic act, which climaxes when Berle performs a stunt with them. Next, out comes the girl singer ("I used to look down her dress, at her cleavage. I got hysterical laughs"). Then Stan Fischer the harmonica virtuoso—who duets with Berle on the drums. The Metropolitan Sextet sings, and Berle introduces himself with his teeth blacked out. He takes his make-up off and talks about his life in show biz. He sings his theme song and says, "Goodnight, thank you. They're waiting for you out there."

After which Berle would go out into the casino and deal some twenty-one for the amusement of the hotel guests.

I always made it a point, any hotel where I was working, that I would never leave the hotel—because *I* was the attraction. There were a lot of folks who would come to Vegas and like to see the personalities. One night, between shows, I grabbed a deck of cards and asked the pit boss if he'd allow me to deal. He said sure. Before you knew it, the table was jammed. I gave a lot of money away—$200, $300, but it was worth it. Just so we could entertain them and keep them in the hotel, so they wouldn't go to another hotel and lose their money. If they're going to lose their money, better they lose it in the hotel I'm playing in.

Berle started a trend that was picked up in the 1950s by Dean Martin and Jerry Lewis, Frank Sinatra, Sammy Davis, Jr., and other entertainers. They all came out and dealt cards.

When Berle arrived in Vegas for the first time he found himself at the Sands craps table within minutes. He quickly won $57,000.

I said, "Where has this been all my life? This is a cinch." I couldn't wait until the first show was over that night to get back out there. But I couldn't, because we had dinner that night with Edward G. Robinson. I said goodbye to [my wife] Ruth and shot some craps before the show. I lost the $57,000 and an additional $60,000, to boot. So, before I went onstage, I had lost $120,000. Being a professional, you smile regardless. I don't think I remembered during the show that I lost it. But I got bawled out by Ruth later. She said, "Why didn't you stop?" I said that asking me to stop is like telling Marilyn Monroe not to show five inches of her cleavage.

And speaking of Miss Monroe: The time was 1960, the place was the Sands, and the occasion was a big birthday party for Rat Packer Dean Martin. Eddie Fischer was working the Desert Inn, and Elizabeth Taylor was in town to visit him. Frank Sinatra was playing the Sands, and he had invited Monroe to come to Vegas and be with him.

The party was held after the first show. Eddie comes up to me and says he has to go do a second show. "Milton, would you be Liz's escort for the evening?" Ruth wasn't in town, so I said, "Sure, I'll take care of it." Then, five minutes later, Frank comes up to me and says he has to go downstairs and do his show, would I please escort Marilyn to the show? What a situation!

Liz is wearing a black turtleneck sweater with her bosoms covered, and Marilyn was wearing a gold lamé with her boobs hanging out. The second show is about to start, and there I am with the two most beautiful Jewish women in the world on both arms [Taylor converted for Fischer; Monroe for Arthur Miller].

We walk into the show room, Liz on one arm, Marilyn on the other side, and Berle in the middle . . . and there was such a roar and a scream, that I said to both of them, "Who says no one knows me?"

I ad-libbed that.

"Are you in here for entertainment or revenge?"

—Milton Berle

135

WAYNE NEWTON

They call him the "Midnight Idol," the "King of the Strip," and "Mr. Las Vegas." No entertainer has been more closely associated with the town. He lives there; he works there more weeks per year than any other musical performer. Wayne Newton—he of the slick black hair and pencil-thin mustache—and Las Vegas, twenty-four hours of glitter, gambling, and adult partying, forever will be intertwined.

How does he feel about that?

"I love it," says Newton, sitting backstage one evening in his black velvet bathrobe with "W.C.N." monogrammed over the breast pocket. "I think it's the greatest compliment in the world. It's funny, because I was reflecting on that recently. It always does surprise me in a very nice way that people so commonly put the two together, almost in the same breath."

Newton is no Vegas native. He was born in Roanoke, Virginia, to parents of American Indian ancestry. He started in show business there at age six. The family moved to Phoenix nine years later, because of Wayne's asthmatic condition. The Newton Brothers—Wayne and Jerry—quickly landed a daily TV show on station KOOL, exposure that led to a five-year contract in

Wayne Newton in performance

the Fremont Hotel's Carnival Lounge, beginning in 1959. There the brothers wowed the crowd with their impeccable musicianship, as they played country ("Jambalaya"), Broadway ("Hey, Look Me Over"), and pop standards ("You're Nobody 'Til Somebody Loves You") with youthful zeal and showmanship.

But Newton admits that when they first came to Vegas, he was disappointed.

> As a child, my image of what Las Vegas was going to be was that the Dunes would appear to be a big sand pile with a door. . . . It was devastating that it wasn't like that. I thought the Flamingo would be shaped like a big bird. It was a child's impression, hearing those names and trying to create mental pictures. Once I got here and realized that the hotels didn't physically look that way, then it was just a matter of plopping down and going to work and falling into the routine of doing six shows a night.

When the Fremont closed its lounge for remodeling in 1963, Wayne got a recording contract with Capitol Records and had big hits with songs like "Danke Schöen" and "Red Roses for a Blue Lady." The Newton Brothers became "Wayne Newton with Jerry Newton" and, eventually,

137

just Wayne Newton. (Jerry continued playing guitar and acting as his brother's comic foil until 1970.)

"Bobby Darin convinced me that no brother act or group act could ever be as big as a single performer, in terms of people's recognition," says Wayne Newton. "If it's a group, your attention span is split up."

The recorded hits stopped coming after Newton's voice changed. But he remained in Vegas, where he continued packing in the audiences. At his peak, he was performing thirty-nine weeks a year for Howard Hughes's Frontier Hotel. (He now does ten to fifteen weeks a year in Vegas and another thirty in Reno, Atlantic City, and elsewhere.)

In 1982 Newton decided to go into business for himself, teaming with veteran casino owner Ed Torres to buy the bankrupt Aladdin. Instead of finding happiness as his own boss, Newton experienced much friction with Torres, and he bowed out of the partnership the following year. Along the way, NBC News reported that Newton had gotten mob money to finance the Aladdin acquisition and that he was friends with a reputed mobster. Newton sued; NBC lost; the case was appealed and the judgment upheld but reduced.

Newton claimed that the NBC story damaged his career and resulted in fewer bookings. That claim notwithstanding, he continues to pack 'em in today—though the show never changes much. Back in 1966 at the Flamingo, the show would close with rollicking versions of "Bill Bailey, Won't You Please Come Home" and "When the Saints Go Marching In." In 1988 at the Las Vegas Hilton, Newton still does "Saints" and stops the show with his fast fiddle playing—as always—on "Orange Blossom Special." These days, instead of "By the Time I Get to Phoenix" and "That's Life," he sings Neil Diamond's "America" and a whole bunch of Elvis tunes ("C. C. Rider," "Suspicious Minds," the "Dixie" medley) and walks off after an hour—only to return and do another hour. Always.

Newton lives ten minutes off the Strip on his "Casa Shenendoah" ranch with his Arabian horses and teenage daughter. After leaving the show, Jerry Newton moved to Tennessee, where he started a car dealership and owned some radio stations. Now retired, he's back in Vegas, living down the street from his brother.

When Wayne Newton is at home, he refuses to sing or play an instrument. "I feel the necessity to keep home away from business and business away from home, because this business can become so totally encompassing and you could live it twenty-four hours a day. That's what causes a lot of people to die so young."

What he will do is *listen* to music. At home, in the car, and up in the air in his helicopter, Newton auditions new songs for the show. His chief criterion: that 99 percent of the audience will be familiar with the tune. When listening to see if a song will work, he'll play it two hundred times in a row. "I judge a song by how it wears on me first," he says.

If it starts to wear on me after four times, I won't do it. The song has to have staying power. There are listening songs and there are performing songs. I did the song from *An Officer and a Gentleman* ["Up Where We Belong"] for a while, but it just went into the toilet—it was a listening song.

SIEGFRIED AND ROY

Siegfried and Roy.
Siegfried and Roy.
Masters of darkness, wizards of joy.
Siegfried and Roy.
Siegfried and Roy.
Masters of darkness, wizards of joy.
Siegfried and Roy, Siegfried and Roy,
SIEGFRIED!!!! AND (Siegfried and Roy, Siegfried and Roy,
Siegfried and Roy, Siegfried and Roy) ROY!!!!
—*Theme song*

Siegfried (standing) and Roy live in a big Jungle Palace near the Strip with twenty-five animals, including tigers, cheetahs, panthers, snakes, an elephant, a horse, and a duck. Within the palace are lots of rare artifacts, like Roy's elephant-tusk bed.

Siegfried and Roy with Neva the tiger at the twenty-one table

OPPOSITE TOP:
Siegfried and Roy onstage

OPPOSITE BOTTOM:
Siegfried and Roy with their manager, Bernie Yuman, in front of the Jungle Palace

As young boys in Germany, Siegfried Fischbacher and Roy Horn used to dream about becoming famous magicians and stars of the great Las Vegas Strip.

Says Roy: "If you can make it there, you can make it anywhere. If you want to be a Pope, you have to go to Rome, but if you want to make it in show business—in our style of show business—you have to go to Las Vegas."

It all began in the summer of 1965, when Siegfried and Roy got jobs on the luxury cruise ship *Bremen*. Bartender Siegfried did a magic act (pulling rabbits out of a hat) in the evening; steward Roy served drinks by day and performed at night with a cheetah.

After watching Siegfried, Roy introduced himself and suggested combining their acts. Instead of pulling a rabbit out of a hat, Siegfried put Roy *and* a cheetah in a box and made them both disappear. The audience loved it.

Siegfried and Roy were in show business.

After working the ships for a couple of years, they got booked in Paris at the *Lido de Paris*. After that engagement, the producers said they were ready for the big time and sent them to Las Vegas, where from 1971 to 1981, they worked in several production shows (*Folies Bergère, Hallelujah Hollywood,* and *Lido*) as specialty acts. In 1981 Kenneth and Irvin Feld of the Ringling Brothers and Barnum & Bailey Circus mounted an entire show around their talents. From 1981 to 1988, their own *Beyond Belief* was the hottest ticket in Vegas; and at this writing, they were scheduled to debut a new show at the Golden Nugget on the Strip, Nugget owner Steve Wynn having signed them to a five-year, $57,000,000 contract.

Siegfried and Roy's calling cards are levitation and the quick disappearance of human beings (pretty women), animals (lions, tigers, elephants, horses), and objects. They also do such traditional tricks as sawing a woman in half. What has made them so popular in Las Vegas is not just that they pull off these illusions—similar tricks are performed every night by other magicians in Vegas show rooms—but that they do the stunts faster than anyone else. The pace is dizzying.

Onstage, the pair is all smiles. At home they bicker and bicker and bicker. Siegfried explains:

Siegfried and Roy get up in the morning and have a two-hour breakfast, and for two hours we sit there and argue. We never agree. But, finally, when we do agree on something, we know we can depend on each other 100 percent, because we know what we're doing.

Siegfried even argues with the animals. It is he who has suffered all the animal bites and scratches; Roy is unscathed.

"Animals love Roy," says Siegfried.

He walks down the street and dogs follow him. He is in harmony with nature. I am in harmony with nature, but I try to challenge it. Roy has a certain feel for animals, which is a gift that I don't even understand after all these years. It's a mystery to me how he does it, but something rubbed off on me, too.

Primarily, Roy's job is to deal with the animals while Siegfried invents the magic stunts. "To be an illusionist you have to be realistic and down to earth," says Siegfried. "Roy is a dreamer. So, alone, Roy is maybe too much. Siegfried would be a little too little. I bring him down, and he brings me up, and we meet in the middle."

Both Siegfried and Roy have a special relationship with an only-in-Las-Vegas character— their manager, Bernie Yuman. A former Miami booking agent for Wayne Cochran and the C. C. Riders, Yuman came to Las Vegas in 1972, where he befriended Paul Lowden, then entertainment director for the Flamingo. Lowden agreed to finance Yuman's personal management company as co-owner. A few days after this, Yuman saw Siegfried and Roy perform at the MGM Grand, signed them, and the rest is history.

"I can tell you with a great deal of objectivity that they are the greatest illusionists in the world," says Yuman. "Their secret is the phenomenon of their relationship with these massive beasts, which results only in one thing—originality."

Always dressed to the nines, with badges on his lapels and gold and silver jewelry on his wrists, Yuman drives a black Corvette bearing a license plate that reads "BLACK." He's been compared to Elvis Presley's legendary manager, Col. Tom Parker, in that he is a master showman who never stops working on behalf of his clients. He is constantly promoting—even though a seat in Siegfried and Roy's show room is one of the hardest things to obtain in town.

"Your laurels stand on their own," he says. "It's tough to go to sleep at night knowing that there is somebody somewhere else making a deal."

Married to Candy Cavaretta, a former Circus Circus acrobat, Yuman's only clients are S&R. What few non-S&R hours there are in his day he keeps very private. Few people know his home telephone number—not even partner Lowden. To reach him, a call must be placed to the Hacienda Hotel, where he has an office; at off-hours the switchboard will try him at home.

For S&R he does a little bit of everything. He oversees their publicity, cuts the deals, books their personal and TV appearances, and, at photo sessions with Siegfried and Roy and the animals, he plays the organ to keep the cats content.

When Siegfried and Roy left the Old Country for Vegas, Roy fell in love with it, but Siegfried didn't feel the same way. "There was no green, no grass, no trees, no birds singing," he says. "It was total culture shock." They rented a house for a year, which they shared with lions, tigers and cheetahs, but they decided that the only way they could be truly happy in Las Vegas would be by creating their own fantasyland.

They bought a house, dubbed it the "Jungle Palace," and planted palm trees and grass. They built a giant swimming pool for the animals. Their housemates in the guarded block-long compound are twenty-two beasts, including tigers, lions, cheetahs, panthers, ducks, elephants, horses, exotic birds, and snakes. Inside the Palace are a great many artifacts, chiefly elephant tusks, masks, clocks, and S&R monograms: a big one adorns the gate to the Palace—inside is a stained-glass S&R window, S&R napkins for drinks served in S&R glasses for visitors in S&R chairs. S&R watches (which simply say "Siegfried and Roy" on the dial) are sold at the show (both magicians own timepieces with photos of themselves on the dial).

They sleep till noon every day; after breakfast Roy takes care of the animals and Siegfried works on new magic tricks. On their day off they practice, practice, and practice. Otherwise, Siegfried and Roy are on that big stage six nights a week with huge smiles on their faces.

"Show business is a very tough business if you don't love it," says Roy.

This is our life. Our life is the stage, and the stage is our life. We live, breathe, and eat show business. As a child, you allowed yourself to dream, and once you become an adult, you become afraid to admit your dreams. You take them, lock them in a little box, and seal them. When they see us onstage we unlock the box and let the dreams come true. So they can dream along with us.

One night, as he watched the show with this writer, manager Yuman pointed out the secret of S&R's success. "Look at that trick," he said. "How's he going to get out of that box? He's out!!! Amazing, isn't it? Unbelievable!!! Speed . . . Execution . . . Triple climax. That's what sets them apart from everyone else. That's why they are the greatest magicians in the history of the business."

After the show, as he walked out to pick up his Corvette (and hand the valet a $20 tip for parking it right in front of the hotel), Yuman continued on the subject of his two clients.

They are the fruition of the American dream. They got off that boat and conquered the country. . . . When they go to Europe, people don't say, "There's Siegfried and Roy," they say, "There's Siegfried and Roy from Las Vegas." It's stamped all over. You see them and you think Las Vegas.

"Sammy told me he'd meet me in temple. I said, how will I know you? He said, I'll be the guy wearing the brown suit."

—Joey Bishop

STARS AND GAMBLING

In "the old days," when "the boys" ran the clubs, the stars were always at the tables between and after the shows. Shecky Greene says that if he had it to do all over again, he would have moved to Iowa—Vegas had a bad effect on him because he couldn't hold his liquor and he couldn't regulate his gambling.

Sammy Davis, Jr., tells of the time he was hired for $50,000 a week to play the New Frontier. He started on a Wednesday, and owed the casino $250,000 by the end of the week. Comedian Joe E. Lewis, one of the biggest draws of the 1950s, played Vegas so often because he was continually in hock to the casinos. He played virtually for free, though they flew him out and gave him a room. His line was that he liked to play Vegas—it was a good opportunity to come out and visit his money.

Says comedienne Phyllis Diller:

If you know how many of the guys went back and played Vegas for nothing, just to pay off their gambling debts. . . . One guy can lose that much to the casino in an hour, so he's paid the entertainment off right there. It's the fastest money in the world—other than oil.

When a comic has just done a brilliant show and then comes to the tables to mingle with the people and gamble, naturally that table fills up around him. Now he has a second audience—he's on. So what can he do but keep gambling? Once you go out to those tables, if you're a man, your ego takes over. Even if you lose $50,000, you can't stop—the people are egging you on. You've got to be their hero. An anonymous person can walk away from that table. But once a star gets out there, forget it. He gets sucked in by his ego. He thinks: My God, they'll think I'm broke. I've got to keep gambling.

I can't imagine a woman going to the tables and doing that. Gambling is a very macho thing. The women are incidental; they're just there for rubbing the temples.

"I never lost a salary, or even half my salary, but I did lose quite a bit," says Bill Cosby, who used to sit in the baccarat pit for hours after his show. "It might come down to $10,000 a night by the end of it." He says that even with their gambling habits, entertainers like Lewis, Harry James, and Eddie Fischer really weren't that bad off.

In a way, it was good news and bad news. You lost x amount of dollars; the good news was you had a job in

Sammy Davis, Jr., in his suite at Bally's, which comes complete with VCR, videodisc player, giant-screen TV, and all the Strawberry Crush you could ever want

two weeks. And it was better to lose it here than back at home. Because at least when you came to work, you knew they were going to pick up your booze and your food and your room, so you could still look good while you were paying off your debts.

Vegas comedian Pete Barbutti got gambling out of his system when his young trio gambled away their entire paychecks on the first day of their week's engagement at the Riviera in 1955.

We went to Bill Miller, who was the entertainment director,

and told him we were in a lot of trouble, and he said, "I tell you what I'll do. I'll give you your money back, but only after you go home and tell your old ladies what you did. I want it to rain on you." And that cured us.

Wayne Newton, who has been playing Vegas since 1959, claims he's never once gambled. "I would not know how to start at a crap table," says the former co-owner of the Aladdin Hotel. "Even when I owned a casino, I couldn't tell you how to play the games. I've worked too hard in my life to see the money go that way. I would rather give it to somebody."

CHAPTER 8

Floor Show

Casinos never advertise that they have the greenest felt on their twenty-one tables or the slowest roulette wheel in town. They advertise entertainment. "Sammy!" "Julio!" "Direct from France— *Lido de Paris!*" "Shecky!" "Girls! Girls! Girls!"

The marquee in front is to let people know what's playing and to differentiate one hotel from the other across the street.

"Ever since Day One, entertainment has been associated with having a good time in Las Vegas," says Sal Murillo, a performer with the *Splash* show. "Entertainment is as much a part of this town as gambling."

At first, Vegas entertainment was in the form of the "floor show." When Sophie Tucker performed at El Rancho and Jimmy Durante played the Fabulous Flamingo in the 1940s and

OPPOSITE:

The "Texas Copa Girls" of the Sands, 1950s

The *Lido de Paris* program at the start of the show's second decade, 1968

The Eighth edition of LE LIDO DE PARIS

LIDO '68

An astonishing all new revue "TOUT PARIS"

The only show in Las Vegas imported from Paris with its original cast!

conceived by PIERRE LOUIS-GUERIN *and* RENE FRADAY

staged and directed by DONN ARDEN

produced by FRANK SENNES

EDDIE O'NEIL *and* his orchestra

SHOW TIMES
8:15 and 12 Midnight
2:30 a.m. Saturday

Costumes created by FOLCO
Art direction HARVEY WARREN
Original music J. P. LANDREAU / *Lyrics* G. ALLEN

Sets designed by H. WARREN & FOST
Musical supervision JIM HARBERT
Orchestrations L. NORMAN & P. DELVINCOURT

Assistants to Donn Arden: CARL JABLONSKI, LARRY MALDONADO

1. TOUT PARIS, NUIT D'ELEGANCE
   a) Femmes et fourrures:
   Les Bluebells de Paris . . . . LES BLUEBELL GIRLS
   Le chic de Paris . . . . LES BELLES DU LIDO
   Les admirateurs . . . . ARDEN BOY DANCERS
   & SINGERS
   Mademoiselle Naughty . . . . **MARYA LINERO**
   b) Voila le Lido:
   Le rythme de Paris . . BOY DANCERS & SINGERS
   Les Miss Lido . . . . BRIONY MERRIMAN
   VALERIE PERRINE
2. TRICKS PLUS PERSONALITY
   RUDY SCHWEITZER
3. SANDS OF ADVENTURE
   a) An Arab camp in the desert:
   The sheik . . . . JACK KASSEL
   Soldiers of fortune . . . . . . ARDEN BOY DANCERS
   & SINGERS
   Chief of the camel caravan . . . . ED. KREIG
   The slave maidens . . . . . . LES BELLES DU LIDO
   The chosen one . . . . **MARYA LINERO**
   THE SAND STORM
   b) The mirage:
   The sheik . . . . JACK KASSEL
   The water sirens . . . . . LES BELLES DU LIDO
   THE POOL OF DREAMS
   c) The harem:
   The exotics . . . . LES BLUEBELL GIRLS
   BOY DANCERS & SINGERS
   Vision of beauty . . . . LES BELLES DU LIDO
   The sheik . . . . JACK KASSEL
   His dream goddess . . . . **MARYA LINERO**
   THE ENCHANTED FOUNTAINS
4. BIG TOP FANTASY
   The balloon clowns . . . . . . ARDEN BOY SINGERS
   LES STEVENS
   The surprise clowns . . . . VALERIE PERRINE
   BRIONY MERRIMAN
   Flying high . . . . **NANCY LEE PARKER**
   and NICKY POWERS
   THE GREAT ICE STAGE

5. FUN IN TYROL
   EVERS & TONI
6. OPIATE D'AMOUR
   a) Rainy night on rue Rivoli:
   The lonely men . . . . . . ARDEN BOY DANCERS
   & SINGERS
   b) Boudoir of Desire:
   The lonely women . . . . LES BLUEBELL GIRLS
7. QUATRE GARCONS SANS SOUCI
   THE REBERTE
8. THE PHANTOM OF THE OPERA
   a) Garden party in Champs Elysees 1890:
   The cream of the Paris society BLUEBELL GIRLS
   LES BELLES DU LIDO
   The boulevardiers . . BOY DANCERS & SINGERS
   The belles of the party . . . BRIONY MERRIMAN
   VALERIE PERRINE
   Their admirer . . . . HARRISON SOMERS
   The prima ballerina . . . . **MARYA LINERO**
   Her lover . . . . LES STEVENS
   b) A dressing room in the Paris Opera:
   The maids . . . . VALERIE CHAPMAN
   HERMIDE KREITZER
   The prima ballerina . . . . **MARYA LINERO**
   The phantom . . . . JACK KASSEL
   c) The grand Paris Opera stage:
   Le ballet blanc . . . . LES BLUEBELL GIRLS
   Le premier danseur . . . . . . CHARLES FERNALD
   or JIM FRANKLIN
   La prima ballerina . . . . **MARYA LINERO**
   The phantom . . . . JACK KASSEL
   THE GREAT FIRE
9. A MAD MOD SYMPHONY 1890
   THE NITWITS
10. C'EST MAGNIFIQUE!
    THE MAGIC STAIRCASE
    Grand Finale . . . . ENTIRE CAST

LES BLUEBELL GIRLS

Joan Gallagher	Boni Lyn	Jean Madsen	Lynette Lewis	Connie Osborne	Gisela Seckleman	Loraine Ibbetson	Valerie Chapman	Irene Morris
Hermine Kreitzer	Margriet Dane	Sylvia Harris	Mary Smith	Judy Ritsko	Rosemary Tall	Caroline Bray	Carol Hall	Audrey Mortimer

LES BELLES DU LIDO

Linda Hall	Angela Sendall	Lilian Silverstone	Sonia Faulds	Gloria Tiffany	Jacqueline Hivet	Anne Chatterton	Renate Schmid	Margo Mansergh
Jane Green	Gillian Brearley	Margaret Mitchell	Janet Clarke	Susan Kinken	Mirha Elias	Ursula Maschmeyer	Maude Chapel	Jan Hall

ARDEN BOY DANCERS

Rod Bieber   Johnny Ritsko   Rick Hamilton   Dan Parker   Charles Fernald   Jim Franklin   Josef Hurban   Mickey Hinton   Ron Alexander

ARDEN BOY SINGERS

Harrison Somers   Bill Carey   Chris Hersey   Jeb Stuart   Les Stevens   Harvey Church   Ernie Knowles   Bill Damien   Kevin Shane

Captain for girls: Audrey Mortimer — for boys: Rod Bieber
All costumes made in Paris by Turpin, Marinette-Aumont, Vicaire, Petit
Interior of Cafe Continental designed by Paul Laszlo I.D.S.A. & Assoc.

Lighting and sound by Eddie White
Company Manager & Stage Construction: Walter Shaner

Donn Arden's 1958 *Lido de Paris*
came complete with topless
showgirls and an onstage waterfall.

'50s, they were always preceded by a line of girls, a comedian or magician, and a specialty act. In 1958, the specs for the Vegas floor show changed radically with the introduction of the so-called spectacular production show: Donn Arden's *Lido de Paris*. It was all production and no headliner. The show was the star.

With the *Lido*'s big spectacle and topless showgirls, the Stardust found they were packing 'em in. And they didn't have to worry about booking stars anymore—some of whom would draw and some of whom wouldn't.

Production shows are expensive, but the costs are rapidly amortized. That's one reason *Lido* has never left the Stardust. It has been playing continuously since 1958.

Show-room stars either travel with their own set or stand solo on the show-room stage, in front of the orchestra. They charge $100,000 to $500,000 for a week's worth of performances. A production show can be mounted for as little as $1,000,000 or as much as $10,000,000. Bally's *Jubilee*, which did cost $10,000,000, opened in 1981. Compared to a $500,000-a-week nut for Frank Sinatra, the floor show pays for itself in twenty weeks.

"The problem with stars is it's all hit and miss," says Sam Distefano, vice president of entertainment for the Riviera, which runs four production shows.

In other words, if you have a Bill Cosby and pay him $500,000 a week, you do very well. But what happens when Bill leaves and you get a $200,000 act—which is still an enormous figure—but you don't fill your show room? When you have the big names, out of the big names, you're going to have names that aren't as big as others. You're going to have slump times.

Today, only four hotels—Hilton, Caesars, Golden Nugget, and Bally's—have a star policy. Every other hotel with entertainment offers a floor show: lots of dancing, pretty ladies, comedy, and magic—the format established by the *Lido*.

"It's very difficult to do a new kind of Vegas show," says Jeff Kutash, producer of the Riviera Hotel's *Splash* revue, "to take subject matter that's contemporary and put it into Las Vegas. How

The Circus Maximus show room at Caesars Palace

do you make it attractive, when you know the reason people are going is to see the cliché?"

Yes, Kutash's show is a revue, with jugglers, animal and balancing acts, and a magician. But the music and dancing are set to a contemporary rock 'n' roll beat. Just to make sure no one's left out, the dancers also swim in giant pools, Esther Williams—style, and the show ends with a big tribute to the U. S. of A., in which all the dancers strike Statue of Liberty poses.

"There's always been a stigma about producing Vegas shows," says Kutash. "But because it's the last profit-making, audience-gathering situation in the world, it has to be respected. The stigma is that it's T&A, old comics and farts. Yesterday's news. I tried at least to bring it to today's news."

"A show like this brings in the masses," says Distefano.

Middle America. When people come to Las Vegas, they generally want to see two shows and a star. They'll always see a star before a production show, because the general public doesn't have any idea what's going on in Vegas until they get in the cab or to the hotel and talk to somebody. You're either a fan of Engelbert or you're not. Somebody tells you a production show is good, you'll try it out.

Not every production show in town follows the French revue guidelines of the *Lido*. There are other kinds—for instance:
• Burlesque: The tassles turn, the baggy-pants comedians tell blue jokes, and the spirit of Harold Minsky lives. But the show really gets going when the lead exotic has her turn in the spotlight at the end. ("Exotics" is what strippers prefer to call themselves.) "It's an art that I cherish," says exotic Bambi, Jr. (a.k.a. Grace Morley). "It's not that I like to take my clothes off. I'm just really

150

into the art of it." Other notable exotics include Tempest and Lynn Chase, a former Miss Nude Universe, whose specialty in *Minsky's Burlesque* was climbing into a giant champagne glass, pouring a bottle of champagne over her nude body, and then stepping to the front of the stage and shaking 'em with everything she's got. Needless to say, the gents up front lapped it up.

- Magic: Siegfried and Roy's *Beyond Belief* mixed the French showgirl and specialty act format with illusions. It worked spectacularly. Virtually every other Vegas show now features magic acts, and several have tried to copy the S&R format with shows like *Abacadabra* and *Magic Magic* (not to be confused with Circus Circus), and *Melinda's Follies Revue*, all built around magic.
- Dance: A line of all-but-nude ladies (or guys) appears on stage, and they get even sexier than the bare-breasted, feather-headdressed ladies of the French shows. They sing, they dance; they bring guys up onstage and sing them into blushing submission. They introduce comedians and magicians. *Crazy Girls, Playboy's Girls of Rock and Roll, The Heat Is On, Dan Sin Dirdy,* and *Hot Lips*—chances are the ads for these shows will feature a lot of uncovered female cheeks and inform you that the show will be a) Sexsational, b) Sexotic, or c) Sexsensual.
- Plays: From the days in 1967 when Caesars showcased *Sweet Charity* with Juliet Prowse, theater has been a staple of the Vegas show room. The Sahara regularly features shows like *A Chorus Line, Ain't Misbehavin',* and *42nd Street* in its show room, and the Union Plaza periodically presents plays like *Norman, Is That You?* and *Natalie Needs a Nightie,* which starred Bambi, Jr., as Natalie. The box office gets really hot when producers can convince an actor with a recently cancelled sitcom—like Sherman Hemsley, who appeared in *Norman*—to star in the show.
- The Revue: The basic variety format without the French touch. The long-running *Holiday Revue*

151

features 1920s-style "flappers" along with the basic magic, jugglers, hulahoop acts, and singers. *Nudes on Ice* is another in a long string of shows from ice producers Bill Moore and George Arnold (*Spice on Ice, Xstasy on Ice, Fantasy on Ice, Ice Fantasy,* and *Razzle Dazzle*), with jugglers, dancers, singers, and, of course, four bare cheeks (ice skaters work in teams) atop skates. "Ice shows are just so unique," says Moore. "When you get away from the *Ice Capades* and *Ice Follies,* do them Las Vegas—style, and get into the nudity, people just love them."

Bonnie Saxe, who produces her daughter Melinda's *Follies Revue,* says the revue really is the ultimate Vegas show. "It's what people expect to see," she says, "Comedy, juggling, the pretty girls, and the whole thing. The revue works best in Vegas because it contains a little of everything. If they can only see one show, it's nice to see a show that includes a variety of things."

• Female Impersonators: Where else but in Vegas could Kenny Kerr as Cher in *Boylesk* and Frank Marino as Joan Rivers in *La Cage* pack 'em in night after night? Both *Boylesk* and *La Cage* feature men impersonating Diana Ross, Judy Garland, and Barbra Streisand. *La Cage* star Marino is a local celebrity as well. He runs his own La Cage Salon, where the "Superstar Special" (precision haircut and style, designer makeover, and a French manicure) costs only $45.

• Dead Impersonators: When Willie Collins wanted to join *Legends in Concert* he was turned

OPPOSITE:
Playboy's Girls of Rock and Roll

Liberace: in the flesh, greeting Elvis Presley, and in effigy, at the Liberace Museum on Tropicana Boulevard

153

down. Yes, they agreed, he did look and sound just like Liberace, but show policy was for impersonators to be hired only *after* the performer had passed away. Two days after Liberace died, Collins had a job performing on the Las Vegas Strip.

Over the next few weeks, Collins got to know Liberace's relatives, who still run the Liberace Museum in town. "It gets a little uncomfortable sometimes, when they say Lee is still playing in Vegas," says Collins, who has a habit of laughing continuously between sentences. "I'm not Liberace, after all. But I really love doing him. I like the mystery that goes behind it, because people like to watch to see if I'm really like Lee in every way."

Other *Legends* stars include Elvis Presley, Marilyn Monroe, Bobby Darin, Louis Armstrong, and Hank Williams.

On the wall in Sal Murillo's office is a list of acts.

• Animal acts	• Bicycle acts
• Girl acts	• Balancing acts
• Acrobatic acts	• Aerial acts
• Jugglers	• Comedy
• Kid acts	• Mime acts

Murillo knows a lot about the act biz. His "Murillo and Uliyses" specialty act is a big hit in *Splash*, where one balances the other on top of his head. But besides that, Murillo is also the top agent in Vegas for specialty acts.

"You can have the entire stage on fire, the *Titanic* sinking, whatever you want, but I'll be damned if it's going to get as much applause as the guy who stands in front of the curtain shooting an apple off somebody's head with a crossbow," says Murillo.

The specialty act is a holdover from vaudeville. It is a freestanding act that can be performed in front of the curtain while the sets are being changed behind the curtain. Every show has at least one. Besides state fairs and the circus, Las Vegas is the only place you'll find the specialty act today.

Acts come to Vegas in every shape, size, and color. Featured at the Holiday Casino are the "Pink People," a male and female magician team with pink hair, eyebrows, mustache, and

Sal Murillo of the Murillo and Uliyses balancing act; he also books specialty acts for Vegas show rooms.

The man with the smile (middle of the back row) is Sam Distefano, the Riviera's vice-president of entertainment. He is surrounded by members of the Riv's shows: *Splash, La Cage Aux Folles,* and *Crazy Girls.*

costumes. Featured in the Flamingo Hilton's *City Lites* shows are the Garza Brothers, three guys who like to paint themselves in gray and act like living statues, climbing over each other in slow motion.

"I get calls all day long from every act in the world," says Sam Distefano.

Everybody dreams about Las Vegas, because a guy can come into town here and be an unknown, and you could put him into a show here, and all of a sudden people like him.

He's from Iowa, he makes $30 on Saturday nights working the Rotary Club. All of a sudden, he comes here and works the talent show, someone sees him, you put him on, and the people love him. So now you've hired him, you're paying him $2,500 a week, which he never made in a year, and he's in show business.

Bobby Berosini didn't come from Iowa, but from Czechoslovakia, where his parents were circus stars. Now he stars in *Lido de Paris* with his four orangutans. "When you come from Czechoslovakia to Austria, you think you are in a fairy-tale land," says Berosini. "It's so different. Then when you go from Europe to America, you really think you're in a fairy-tale land—the cars, the people, everything's so fast. *Then* when you go from New York to Las Vegas—look out."

At the beginning of the act, Berosini comes out, tells some jokes and trys to get the orangutans to do things for the audience. Eventually they cooperate, but first they will give him the finger and fart a lot.

"Let me tell you," he says,

you can do triple somersaults, you could juggle twenty hoops, but when you make people laugh, that's the ultimate in show business. You can disappear here and disappear there, but you make people laugh and they carry it with them for the rest of their life.

Bobby Berosini, who works with orangutans nightly in *Lido de Paris*

Berosini upstaged

OPPOSITE:
Vegas audiences just *love* feathers.

Berosini, who lives near the Strip with wife Joan, houses the apes in a special $250,000 Greyhound bus, where they eat bananas, French fries, and cornflakes, and watch TV ("Simon and Simon," "Magnum P.I.," and cartoons). He says he couldn't do a solo act, because he's very insecure. "I'm almost like an orangutan myself. I can speak to the people, and they can't; that's the difference. What they can't say, I say. We have everything in common. We're both insecure and introverted. We don't make friends easy."

Producers Bill Moore and George Arnold use plenty of specialty acts in their shows, but, for them, the most important ingredient in a show's success is old music. "Nostalgia," says Moore. "We always add some of that into the shows, because the music is so familiar. People don't necessarily remember the titles, but the ear does. There's so much old music on Muzak that it just becomes second nature for you to listen to it." Old music means the classics: Gershwin, Porter, Rodgers and Hart. "Rock 'n' roll isn't our bag. It's so fleeting. It doesn't last." But when asked to sum up the basic ingredients necessary for a Las Vegas show, Moore uses one word:

Boobies. . . . I always think you have to give the people what they expect. Even in the 1980s, when we're living in these crazy times and people are almost naked in the streets. People come to Las Vegas and want to see nudity onstage. There's something sensuous about the whole thing. After the curtain goes up and you see it, you forget that it's there, because the costumes and the theater are so beautiful, it's almost overwhelming.

THE PRODUCER: DONN ARDEN

The show opens with a big production number featuring tall, topless, smiling showgirls, followed by nostalgic tributes to Cole Porter and George Gershwin, then turns by magicians, jugglers, and specialty acts, as well as staged disasters like the explosion of the *Hindenburg*, and then another production number to top off the evening. It's the basic Las Vegas "production" show, as invented by producer Donn Arden.

"He is the genius," says Bill DeAngelis, Arden's former executive producer. "He *is* Las Vegas entertainment."

Since his first show premiered at the Desert Inn in 1950 with Edgar Bergen and Charlie McCarthy headlining, a day hasn't passed without at least one Arden show (such as *Hello America, Hallelujah Hollywood, Lido de Paris,* and *Jubilee*) playing in Vegas.

Showgirls and disasters have been his calling cards: tits and glitz, along with a stage re-creation of the San Francisco earthquake and the explosion of the *Hindenburg*.

Smoke, fire, collapse, screaming, panic—people love it, when they're not involved in it. With disasters you can become your own Steven Spielberg. . . . People like to be amazed and leave the theater talking about how you did it. The first *Lido* show was the first time anyone in this country in any theater ever saw a hundred thousand gallons of water a minute pouring into a swimming pool. . . . It was . . . a waterfall effect; you open the curtain, and there's all this water gushing out.

A show was just another show before Arden came to Vegas and added spectacle and drama. "He dared to do dramatic things which had never been done before," says Fluff LeCoque, a former Arden showgirl who now serves as his company manager for *Jubilee*. "He always built numbers around me where I would have to scream. I was being raped or dying or drowning. But he also brought very tender touches of beauty. Somewhere in his productions there's always that wonderfully tender moment of beauty."

But no one ever said the Donn Arden audition had any moments of tenderness. He's been described as a DeMille-like dictator, sitting in the back of the theater with his microphone, yelling nasty things at the throngs assembled to audition.

Legendary Vegas show producer
Donn Arden

Hello, America

I think I can be very nice, and I think I can also be very mean. You know, when you advertise auditions, you state that you really want professionals. Too many people walk in off the street—maybe they're working down the street in the pancake house flipping flapjacks and decide to come in and waste your time and say they're a singer. According to the equal rights thing, we have to audition everybody, but you know within the first eight bars whether they can sing or not. Sometimes you can tell in two. And the same thing applies to dancers. There's no such thing as a natural dancer. The dancers I hire absolutely must have proper ballet training. They must have jazz training. You have no time, even in ten- to twelve-hour rehearsals, to teach a girl who's never had training how to dance.

Donn Arden inspecting his feathers

We specify no girls under five foot eight; I can't tell you how many girls five-four show up. But we have to audition them, even when there's no possibility of us hiring them. They're wasting their time, but they just enjoy having fun at our expense.

So you finally have to say, "Sorry, darling, I can't use you" or "I hope you grow up one of these days" or "Eat more potatoes." You try to be polite, but there's some times when they're evil, when they won't leave, when they want another chance. You have no time to put up with that, and you must say, "Will you please leave my theater?"

Arden could also be quite hard on the "kids" at rehearsal, but DeAngelis says it is all mostly for effect. "He would do that to get the best out of people, because, for some unknown reason, when you're annoyed and you get upset inside, you hit back. He'd get more talent out of people by being nasty to them." The dancers wondered how Arden got away with it. "He would say things to some of those girls that weren't to be believed," says Jimmy Baron, a former Arden dancer.

> "Get your nose fixed!" "Get your ears pinned back!" "You look terrible!" These were the days of the hoods always being around, and they were going out with many of the girls. They were going to take him out back and beat him up once, but one of the other bosses said, "Go ahead and do it, if you think you can come back tonight and produce the show."

Arden was born in St. Louis, where he was tap dancing by age fifteen and, by twenty, was running dance groups that played clubs in many cities. In 1950, "the boys" who ran the clubs in Cleveland told Arden about the new casino—the Desert Inn—they were building in Vegas. They wanted Arden to do the floor shows. He could hardly refuse. And a Vegas career was born.

> In those days I was running a girl factory. I was doing shows in Cincinnati, St. Louis, Philadelphia, New York, Chicago, and Montreal. At the Desert Inn we didn't do big production numbers. What we did was an opening, a center production, and a finale, and we had a couple of acts in between. We were basically book covers for the shows.

From that basic floor show came the "spectacle" of the 1960s and the scenes of destruction that have become Arden's trademark. When he brought the *Lido* from Paris to Vegas in 1958, he introduced a new look for the showgirl. She was taller, a better dancer, and she wore a lot of feathers on her head. Over the years, the headdresses have gotten heavier (some weigh thirty pounds or more), and, over the years, Arden has become quite an expert on the subject of feathers. "There is such a difference between a good feather and a bad feather," he says.

> The good feathers used to come from Europe; now they come from Africa. The woman I deal with in Paris owns a couple of ostrich farms in Africa. She goes around plucking all those feathers out of their tails. Then she cleans them and dyes them and sticks them in a boxcar.

Arden always has two shows playing in Vegas—the *Lido* at the Stardust and *Jubilee* at Bally's—as well as the original *Lido* in Paris. He doesn't ever have to worry about money. Three checks—for the three shows—come in the mail to his Palm Springs home each week. (He also has a waterfront adobe in Mission Viejo, California.) The bosses at first wanted to give Arden a lump sum for his shows. "But with my drinking and gambling, I never believed in that. I'd rather have the security of a weekly paycheck." It's a nice annuity when a show—like *Lido*—runs for over thirty years. *Jubilee* has been playing since 1981.

Arden has found that the new owners of the hotels want him to produce shows for less money. *Jubilee* cost $10,000,000; the new breed of bosses feels half that should buy a good show. After all, *Splash* at the Riviera only cost $1,000,000, and it packs 'em in every night.

But $10,000,000 is the minimum Arden needs for a new show.

> My business, it seems like it's going out of fashion. I'm known to be an expensive guy, and it just costs money to put these shows on. You spend money; you make money. Of course, I can put them in a bikini and stick a feather in their head and one bracelet on the arm and little earrings, but that isn't the glamorous show that I do. The things that make my show look right are expensive.

"Look at the Strip. The Dunes, the Desert Inn, the Sands, the Sahara, the Aladdin. My God, Moses went the wrong way. *This* is the promised land."

—Jack Carter

OVERLEAF:
Donn Arden's *Jubilee*, the most expensive show ($10 million) in Vegas history

SHOWGIRLS

She is nearly six feet tall, with a frozen, thick red smile, wears thirty pounds of feathers on her head, and has the biggest pair of eyelashes you ever saw. She is the Las Vegas showgirl, a fixture of the Strip ever since the days of the "floor shows" at the Desert Inn in 1950.

Back then, all the hotels had a "line" of girls to call their own. They opened and closed the show and kicked up their heels: the "Flamingoettes," the "Texas Copa Girls" at the Sands, and the "Desert Inn Beauties." They would work two or three shows a night in the show room and a show or two out in the casino, where "the boys" asked them to "mix and mingle" with the gamblers between and after the shows.

"Certainly, you weren't expected to sleep with the guys," says Jeanie Malone, a former 1950s D.I. "Beauty." "That was up to you, but you better be discreet about it."

She suggests that "the boys" who ran the hotel at the time wouldn't take too kindly to the idea of their showgirls moonlighting in the world's oldest profession, because they had their own "stable" of ladies who did that for a living.

"We were not there for that purpose. We were there to decorate the casino. And some of the girls were very good at the game—which was to get the guys to give you the chips without going to bed with them."

Those were the days when the prettiest women in the world could be hired as showgirls, because all they had to do was walk across the stage and kick in unison. At the time, being a good dancer wasn't a prerequisite for the job, and women were eager for the work, because the fringe benefits were astronomical. After the shows, the girls looked like Hollywood starlets, in beautiful gowns and furs. Says veteran Vegas producer Bill Moore (*Nudes on Ice, City Lites*): "They made so much money in those days that they could supply their own," he says. "When these gamblers won money, it was like easy come, easy go."

And how much were the girls making?

"Untold," says Moore. "It was that high. I remember them coming and tipping their purses out on the dressing-room table, and the chips would be piled sky high. Hundreds of dollars in chips."

It's not too hard to figure out why these girls did so well; they were knockouts. "We had showgirls that were showgirls," says Bill DeAngelis. "They don't make showgirls like they had in those days. Just the way they walked made you want to eat them alive. You don't get that feeling anymore with showgirls. It's just not the same."

What happened? The introduction, in 1958, of the so-called spectacular shows like *Lido de Paris* required better dancers. Producers could no longer just pick the prettiest gals in town; they

A *Jubilee* showgirl

The Flamingoettes

OPPOSITE:
Lido de Paris showgirl Lora
Chamberlin

Backstage at *Jubilee* with Fluff
LeCoque

TOP RIGHT:
Fluff LeCoque, now company manager for the *Jubilee* show, was a
showgirl back in 1960.

168

had to have dancing talent. They also had to be able to learn Arden's famous "showgirl walk."
Arden explains:

> There's a certain way a girl can walk, particularly when you're going across the stage.
> By simply twisting the foot, it swings the pelvis forward, which is suggestive and sensual.
> When you're crossing your feet and you're going across, if you twist right and swing
> that torso, you get a revolve going in there that's just right.

Along with the showgirl walk and a better class of dancer, *Lido* ushered in another major
production change: the topless showgirl. There are none in Atlantic City, where it's illegal to
dance nude, and very few production shows in Reno or Lake Tahoe. So Vegas is just about the
only place you'll find her.
And how hard is it to find ladies to dance topless?
"Usually, when kids come here to work, if they have never worked topless before and they
have the facilities to do it, I ask them if they would like to work topless, and they say no,"
according to former—covered—showgirl Fluff LeCoque.

> Then, somewhere down the line, if they're here long enough, they realize it's not so
> terrible, because you're not degrading yourself. The girls aren't presented in a cheap
> way, like in a strip club. You can't say it's not meant for sexual attraction, but it's not
> meant to be pornographic, it's not meant to degrade the girls. It's meant to beautify
> them. . . . It's as though you were in a picture frame, and you don't have to react
> to people's reactions to you, seeing you nude. You're presenting yourself as a thing
> of beauty, and that's not embarrassing. It's also a compliment just to be asked to
> dance nude, because it means they have a nice body, and they'll make more money.

Besides dancing ability, what are the producers and company managers looking for at those infamous Vegas showgirl auditions? Depends on whom you ask.

"Big boobies," says producer Moore. "We like big boobies, because, in general, we think men like big boobies."

"Small and firm," says LeCoque.

We want the girls to have a nice body and small, virginal bosoms. We don't like girls that are big busted, because they can be distracting when they dance. If all they did was walk, then you could have girls that are a little more well-endowed, but not when they're bouncing around. That's offensive.

Why present topless dancers at all?

"For the shock value," says LeCoque. "Even in this day of *Playboy* and *Hustler*, people are still shocked by it."

But there has been some debate during the last few years about whether nudity is still needed. When producer Jeff Kutash put *Splash* into the Riviera, he deliberately designed it as a "covered" show to attract a wider audience, families included. The Flamingo Hilton's *City Lites* covers 'em up—in the summertime—for the same reason. The showgirls in Siegfried and Roy's show used to dance topless every night; now they bare their bosoms during the last show only. Siegfried, too, wants to attract families:

People come from all over the world to see the show. If we have topless dancers [underage audience members] couldn't get in. That's not right. Topless showgirls are left over from the beginnings of Las Vegas. Today, when you can turn on cable TV and see stuff like that all the time, you don't need to come to Las Vegas to see topless women.

Six nights a week in *Melinda's Follies Revue* Suzanne Saxe struts across the stage in a bikini and heels, yanks her top off, and pretends to sunbathe onstage. Later in the evening, in a number called "Nasty Girls," she wears a black wig and an outfit straight out of Frederick's of Hollywood—a sort of Victorian swimsuit, with her breasts hanging out on top.

Melinda, who calls herself the "First Lady of Magic," levitating her sister in a suite at the Landmark Hotel

The producer who signed her for this assignment is her mother, Bonnie Saxe, a former *Folies Bergère* (covered) dancer, who is also the producer of *Melinda's Follies Revue*, which stars Suzanne's (covered) sister, Melinda, known as "The First Lady of Magic." (Melinda makes VW Beetles and live doves disappear and does a lot of magical dancing; the most she exposes is two cheeks on the Landmark's marquee, ads, and onstage.)

What's it like watching your daughter strut her stuff topless onstage every night?

I don't even think about it. She has a pretty body. I accepted dancing topless when I was in shows. When Suzanne first started dancing topless [in Lake Tahoe shows], she asked me what I thought, and I told her it was totally up to her. If it wasn't vulgar or anything, and she felt comfortable with it, then she should go for it.

The concept of the showgirl goes back to 1869 and the premiere of the *Folies Bergère* in Paris. By 1918 the Folies showgirl was topless. American producer Flo Ziegfeld brought the—covered—showgirl concept to Broadway in the 1920s with his "Ziegfeld Follies." Topless, she became a fixture of post–World War II French shows like *Lido de Paris* before coming to Vegas in 1958, the year a topless showgirl first walked across a Vegas stage.

For all of the talk about glamour and excitement, the Vegas showgirl has one of the lowest paid jobs in town. The busboy in the dealer's dining room makes more money—and works fewer hours. Showgirls work six nights a week for an average weekly salary of $450 as a covered dancer, $500 for working topless.

Being a showgirl today "is for the birds," says producer Arden. "It's a factory, it's a short life, and I'm the first to say it. The kids today, if they're taking my advice, are going to the university. The kids should know it's a disappearing business."

But LeCoque says that even if the money is less than it was in the mix-and-mingle days, working conditions are much better. "It's more professional," she says. "The girls have insurance now, two weeks' vacation every year, and one day off a week. We never used to have a day off. We worked every day. And they have six-month contracts now. When I was working there was no such thing as job security."

Just don't expect to get rich.

"Come into this town with a realistic view," says Bally's showgirl Lisa Browder. "If you come here expecting diamonds, furs, and stardom, forget it. You'll be sorely disappointed. If you come here for a steady dance job, this is one of the steadiest."

She will admit that all showgirls share a common dream. "That we will become rich and famous and be discovered. You know, the Hollywood story."

Yet it's only happened once—with Valerie Perrine, who went on to fame in such movies as *Lenny* and *Slaughterhouse Five*. She was lead showgirl in Arden's *Lido* and Desert Inn shows. Arden recalls working with her.

Valerie Perrine is one of the few Las Vegas showgirls whose chorus-line work opened doors to a movie career.

She was a secretary in Phoenix, fresh and adorable. She said she wanted to go into show business. All she had to do was learn how to walk beautifully and carry beautiful costumes. She lisped like mad, but she was completely excited and enchanted about being in show business. Then one day she walked up to me and said, "Mr. Arden, I have something I want to show you," during auditions for a new show. A friend of hers put on a tape of music, and out she came—nude. I was stunned and shocked. I never dreamed she would do that. Her breasts were sensational, and her torso! Wonderful! And she had learned to dance, too.

She stayed with the show several years, and I wanted to send her to the *Lido* in Paris, but she said to me, "Donn, I'm going to Hollywood. I'm going to try." I figured, with her luck and stamina, she could do it.

Well, there is one other famous showgirl alumna. Goldie Hawn—who didn't dance topless—worked only a few weeks before Arden fired her. "She was a scatterbrain and a giggle queen," he says. "She was way too skinny then, though now I find her beautiful and female. I don't think she's really classically beautiful—but she comes across in the same way that Barbra Streisand does."

Producer Arden isn't highly demanding just about the female body. He's also "very fussy about buns" when he hires the showboys. "Boys have to strip for me, too," he says, "because I always have a number or two to please the women in the audience, so that they can see a hunk of man." He requires "firm and tight" buns. "It's amazing how many boys' buns are droopy—they can sag right down to their knees."

In the world of Donn Arden, no bun should ever droop, and ladies should be amply filled out.

THE SHOWGIRL: LISA BROWDER

Lisa Browder grew up in a small, dusty Texas town, which she dreamt of leaving for a glamorous dance career. She took the plunge in 1976, after watching a TV special about Vegas featuring revue dancers. She said, "I can do that," packed her bags, and drove out to Vegas the next day.

She quickly found a job as a pool waitress at Circus Circus and went on auditions as often as she could. Three months later, she passed. The job: a topless dancer in *Casino de Paris* at the Dunes Hotel.

They said, "You do realize that all the positions are topless. Does that bother you?" Well, here I've been trying to get a job for three months. I'm not going to turn around and say I won't do it if I have to be topless. Besides, I had seen *Lido,* and I thought it was pretty. I didn't find anything degrading about it.

But she was nervous.

The first night before the show, you worry and worry. Then you have so much to think about—"What's the jewelry to go with the next costume?" "Do I remember the steps?" "Oh, don't forget this part, where the boys cross through." So many little things to remember during the show that you don't think about it until it's over, and then you suddenly go, "Oh, I did it." And, after that, it's no problem.

I did some nude modeling for art classes in college, and this is a piece of cake compared to that. I never think about dancing topless, unless we get some country bumpkin sitting up front who thinks he's at the Palomino Club [a local strip joint] and starts making comments that you can hear. I'm not embarrassed for me, but I do want to buy him a subscription to *Penthouse* magazine and send him up to his room.

"You see a lot of crazy people here. When I say 'crazy' I mean crazy for gambling. I was coming through the casino and I saw a man yelling at his wife. He said, 'Alice, I'm ashamed of you. You lost $300 on the slot machines.' She said, 'But what about you, Charlie? You lost $4,000 on the crap tables.' He said, 'Yeah, but I know what I'm doing.'"

—Milton Berle

Since showgirls wear the feathers, wigs, and giant eyelashes, it is theoretically possible for them to walk down the street after the show without being recognized by the people who have watched them in the showroom. Theoretically. But not really. "Even if I don't have any makeup on, I'll walk down the street and hear people say, 'There goes one.' I can't figure out how they know. I don't know what it is, but people seem to spot us."

Most showgirls have lives outside of the casinos—primarily because they work a short career that will end in their thirties. They go to school, work in stores, run businesses. (Browder volunteers at a local hospice.) But a lot of tourists still think they're hookers on the side.

"You have a lot of nice people here in town who understand what you do for a living," says Browder, who has been appearing in Bally's *Jubilee* since 1985.

They'll come by your table and say "nice show," and you appreciate that. Then there are the ones who make tacky little comments, who stare at you; and you can hear them discussing whether or not you're a hooker. And, now and then, if you happen to stop in a bar after work with some of your friends, somebody will come over and offer you money. And people wonder why we walk through the casinos looking very solemn, looking very conceited. We walk through that way to discourage people, to discourage that idiot who's going to walk up and say, "How much money?" You want to punch his face in.

Lisa Browder and company are hard-working women who come to the hotels every night at seven, do two shows, and leave at one A.M. Six nights a week. Not exactly a glamorous life. "It's very rare when we do anything that is glamorous," says Browder.

Any show—as beautiful as this show is—can get tiring night after night. The finale is always glamorous. You can't help but feel glamorous in Bob Mackie designer dresses. They're just too pretty. The rest of the numbers, you really dance, you really work, you sweat. You don't feel too glamorous with sweat pouring all over you. But, every now and then, there is something to make it really neat.

One night, Sammy Davis came to see the show and sent champagne back for the entire cast and then came back to greet us. That was special. You almost feel like part of the show biz family.

Showgirl Lisa Browder

Lisa Browder at home, without the makeup or feathers

Sammy and Wayne and Engelbert get to sing different songs occasionally, but the dancer in the production show dances the same steps every single night.

"Yes, it gets boring now and then, but it's what I'm trained to do," she says.

Entertainment people are really different from normal people—we don't say "people who work nine to five," we say *normal* people. Most of the people I went to high school with all got married and had babies and didn't move more than a hundred miles from home. When you get together with them, you talk about how much a washing machine is selling for at Sears. I've tried to figure out what is the difference— how did I end up so different—but I've never been able to figure it out. The point is, we like doing this. This is our home.

THE SPECIALTY ACT: MURILLO AND ULIYSES

Some people in show business have it easy—all they have to do to pay the bills is sing a couple of songs or tell some jokes. But not Sal Murillo and Uliyses Reyes.

They are partners in what is called a "balancing act." Murillo stands on his own two feet as Reyes does a basic headstand on top of his partner's head. That's the opening number. Jokes—in many different languages—are the middle of the act. The finale is a death-defying teeth clencher: Murillo and Reyes each hold a giant curved knife between their teeth. Reyes does the headstand again, and they walk the stage together without cutting each other up. It's a visual extravaganza that can only be appreciated onstage; specialty acts like this don't work on television.

The mandate for Murillo and Uliyses—as with every other specialty act in town—is to wow the crowd with a ten- to fifteen-minute act in front of the curtain while the stage is being reset. That's what Murillo and Uliyses do every night for the *Splash* show.

"My dream was always to come here," says Murillo. "People would always say to me, 'You are a Las Vegas type of act.' I never knew what they meant. Now I do. We didn't belong in the circus. We're entertainers. In the circus, everything is *watch me, look how difficult this is.* But we just do it."

Murillo, whose parents had a lion-taming act, lived most of his early life in Mexico and Italy, working the circus. "I did trampoline, juggling, high wire, the works," he says. "My dad's theory was, the more you know in the circus world, the more you'll be able to succeed.

"I was a jack of all trades and a master of none. I hated it all. Circus work was hard labor. There was rigging, props, lugging equipment all over the place."

Reyes was born in Venezuela; his family moved to Canada, where dad Alfredo Reyes worked a balancing act called Rolan and Rolan, basically the same sort of act Murillo and Uliyses do today. The act played the Seattle World's Fair in 1964 and Vegas for nine years, as part of shows like *Vive Les Girls* and *Casino de Paris* at the Dunes.

It was watching Rolan and Rolan at the Utah State Fair in 1967 that inspired Murillo finally to leave the circus. "I said to myself, someday I'll do something like that. That's the direction for me."

As Murillo related this story over French dip at the Riviera coffee shop, Reyes turned to his partner and asked him a question about the lightbulb that went on in his head in 1967. When he made the decision about being a balancer, did he decide whether he wanted to be on top or on bottom?

Murillo laughed, but declined to answer. He did explain that he quickly put together a balancing act, patterned after Rolan and Rolan. Things, however, didn't work out with his partner, and Murillo approached the elder Reyes, seeking permission to work with his then fourteen-year-old son. The answer was no. But Murillo persisted and, finally, Reyes relented after his son turned fifteen and a half. "He gave us twenty or thirty years of insider's information, so that we didn't have to make the same mistakes," says Murillo.

Uliyses Reyes had not been interested in a performer's life. He had started gymnastics at age five, choosing to stay inside the gym while all the other kids were playing outdoors. He quit in disgust after a few years because his father, a strict disciplinarian, continually frustrated him. Then, one night, the elder Reyes's partner fell asleep at the wheel of his car. The accident put him in a wheelchair for life. Uliyses decided to get back into the business—to make his father "proud of me."

For Murillo and Uliyses, however, it was very tough at the beginning. "We worked every toilet in the world," says Murillo, "in Europe, Mexico, Brazil, Peru. . . . We lived on crackers and ketchup and made soup out of it. That's how hungry we were. We practiced every day for seven years. We were pumping gas in San Jose and training by day."

The turning point came when they played the Los Angeles County Fair in Pomona, opening for Kenny Rogers. An agent saw them and suggested they try Vegas. He booked them into the *Jubilee* show at the MGM Grand for a while and then they moved to the *Folies Bergère* at the Tropicana. At that point, Murillo and Uliyses became more than just a stunt act; they are different from most specialty acts in that they talk to the audience and tell jokes. Because of their multinational backgrounds, they can speak to the audience in many tongues.

"The key to our success was when we started talking," says Murillo. "We had had no showmanship. All the balancing in the world isn't half as difficult as the delivery of a good comic line."

Alfredo Reyes was so proud of their rapport with the audience, he said to his son: "If I ever see you practicing another stunt, I'll break off your legs." Which brings us to the obvious question: Why do Murillo and Uliyses balance themselves on top of each other?

"It's the satisfaction of having achieved one of my goals," says Reyes, "to do it in Las Vegas, to be one of the top acts in town. It's very fulfilling to be admired by people. It's an

Murillo and Uliyses go head to head.

ego boost. It's one of the few jobs where you really get recognition. The public sees you and compliments you."

End of story? Not quite. Murillo says he and his partner now make "more than a hotel president" ($150,000 to $200,000 a year) and work only twenty-five minutes a night, six nights a week.

It is, however, extremely grueling work, which requires lots of preparation. Every night before they perform, they work out backstage with weights. They wipe the sweat off, put on their blue tuxes, run out onstage, and sweat all over again. The next morning, each awakes and goes to his day job. Murillo is the president of Unique Entertainment, a theatrical management firm that represents some two hundred acts, mostly in Vegas, but also in Italy, Japan, China, South America, and Germany. Reyes runs the Upstage Hair Company, a hair salon frequented by showfolk.

They decided they needed sidelines after suffering the perils of balancing: concussions, shoulder injuries, and bloody teeth. "*Splash* is a hobby," says Murillo. "We've had so many injuries that we figured we better prepare for the future, in case anything ever happens."

THE SHOW SINGER: ALLYN GAMBLE

What a great Vegas name: Allyn Gamble—the show singer who never wagers. A former lounge crooner and Miss Maine of 1971, she came to Vegas on a lark and ended up working in all the really big shows—*Folies Bergère*, *Lido de Paris*, and *City Lites*. Hers is the world of "'S Wonderful," "Girls Just Want to Have Fun," and "42nd Street"; of sequined gowns, "where ya from?" and gambling jokes.

Vegas show singer Allyn Gamble

I enjoy the freedom singing in a show gives me. I can present myself as Allyn Gamble, a person. I'm not just a singer in the show. That's nice, because when people leave, they know who I am. In some production shows, by the time you come out and take your bow at the end, they're saying, now what did she do?

The singer ended up on the West Coast after marrying a Navy pilot stationed in California. He was in the air more often than on the ground, so they split, and she thought about what she wanted to do with the rest of her life. Gamble saw an ad for "girl singers" to audition for producer Donn Arden's *Hallelujah Hollywood* show at the MGM Grand and decided to give it a try.

It was one of those famous Arden auditions. The producer was in the back with his microphone, women were coming up onstage, and he was giving them about five seconds each. "I sat there for two hours at that audition, terrified to get onstage because of the things he was saying to people. 'You should be a plumber; get off my stage.' 'Lose forty pounds and come back and see me.'" But he let Gamble sing her song ("Put on a Happy Face") all the way through and then announced to the crowd: "Now, *that*, ladies and gentlemen, is a singer."

Her career as a show singer began the next day.

Two years later, she moved to the Stardust, for a much larger role in Arden's *Lido de Paris*, as the lead singer. "It was so exciting," she says.

When you work in a show like that, they spend millions and millions of dollars on all the details. They measure every piece of you, down to your fingers. They cut a piece of your hair and send it to Paris, and you get a costume that matches your hair color.

I watched the first show and didn't even notice the girls were topless. It was the most incredible thing I had ever seen. And working with those animals! [Siegfried and Roy were an act in the show at the time.] I used to get the extreme thrill of standing ankle deep in camel shit. . . . It didn't feel very good. And the people in the audience were usually more entertained by watching the camel shit roll around the floor than by watching what was going on.

176

She stayed with the show for only six months because of numerous run-ins with the entertainment director of the hotel, reputed mob front man Frank "Lefty" Rosenthal.

> He wanted me to have a lot of interaction with him, but I wasn't interested. I figured fourteen shows a week was enough. I didn't want to do another one at the bar after the show with Lefty and his boys. I didn't feel I had to play footsie with them every night.

She quit and joined the *Casino de Paris* show at the Dunes. When the show closed, Gamble became a lounge lizard, performing at the rollicking Cleopatra's Barge at Caesars and the Sahara's Casbah. "Lounges are a completely different atmosphere," she says. "In a show room, at least [the audience is] prepared to see a show. In a lounge, they're basically there to be with each other."

Gamble preferred the show room. After two years of lounges, she went back to shows—two years at *Folies Bergère* and then *City Lites* at the Flamingo Hilton.

Her problems with pushy males didn't end at the Stardust. A certain Japanese tourist gave her a night she'll never forget. She was singing "Ring Them Bells" (the song about the slots) in *City Lites*.

> In the opening segment of the show, I always go down the stairs in between tables and shake hands. One night, there was this large Japanese group sitting in front. They were all very relaxed. They had their coats off and shirtsleeves rolled up, which was very unusual, because Japanese businessmen tend to be very proper. I walked up to this one man and shook his hand. He proceeded to take his other hand, reach up, and grab my boob. Not just a little grab—but he climbed on that thing and was shaking it up and down and around. So I turned around and decked him. The whole audience went *woooo*. I thought my job was over. But I just kept on singing.

She also kept her job.

Vegas turned out to be good for Gamble. But she says it is a lonely town for a single woman.

> Because of the hours we work. For a town that supposedly has some of the most eligible bachelors, I haven't met too many of them. It's a difficult town to meet people. The kind of people I meet when I go out in the daytime are musicians or dancers (who tend to be gay)—the people who do what I do. I tend to be attracted to somebody who's more on the normal scale of life, like a businessman. I'm more interested in someone with a normal life-style rather than crazy hours like me.
>
> It's really hard to go out with anybody, because they're ready for the sack at nine-thirty, and I have another show to do. And you only have one night off a week.

THE ELVIS EMULATOR: TONY ROI

He was the greatest draw ever to play a Vegas show room. He was the man who sang "Viva Las Vegas" twice a night for thirty days in a row. He was the King of Rock and Roll.

But Elvis bombed at first. He played the New Frontier in 1956, at the height of his fame, but gamblers weren't interested. He returned in 1969, as the second act to perform at the International Hotel. There wasn't an empty seat.

He continued to play the hotel (later known as the Las Vegas Hilton) in month-long engagements, three to four times a year until his death in 1977.

Presley's Vegas era was the time of karate chops and the big acoustic guitar that led the band; big, white, studded jumpsuits and sweaty scarves for the ladies in the front row; "My

Tony Roi sings "Viva Las Vegas" six
nights a week.

Way," "C. C. Rider," and the "Dixie" medley (also known as "Glory, Glory, Hallelujah"). It is the Vegas era that Elvis emulators choose to emulate.

The Presley influence lives on at the Hilton, with a statue of the performer and one of his guitars encased in front of the show room. Stars of the Hilton show room get to stay on the twenty-eighth floor, in a special wing called "The Elvis Suite." On most days, Presley's former manager, Col. Tom Parker, can be found at the Hilton playing the slot machines.

Vegas was where Elvis used to take Priscilla in the middle of the night, hopping in the van, popping some pills, staying up all night, and sleeping all day. His image lives on at Strip souvenir shops, on towels, posters, postcards, and liquor decanters. He's also the main attraction of *Legends in Concert*, a show at the Imperial Palace that features impersonations of dead stars.

Tony Roi is the current *Legends* King. He was preceded by a man who called himself simply Jonathan. After Jonathan fell in love with another member of the cast—the woman who emulated Marilyn Monroe—they both quit, got married, and moved to Hawaii.

Legends producer John Stuart found Roi in Florida, playing with a Top 40 act that used to end the show with a tribute to the King. Stuart offered him the opportunity to move west and be a Vegas star, but Roi turned him down at first.

179

Julian Albulet backstage in his Circus
Circus dressing room

I said I'd never wear a jumpsuit. At the time, there were all these guys with heavy makeup and thick glasses, trying to do an Elvis act. I just didn't think they looked or sounded anything like Elvis. But then this lady who knew Elvis very well told me that I would be doing his name justice by doing the act. So I changed my mind.

I've always looked like Elvis. And I always sounded like him, too. I could sing Latin and still sound like Elvis.

So Roi bought himself five $2,000 jumpsuits, packed up, and headed west with his wife. Pretty soon he was singing "Viva Las Vegas" every night.
"I was always a big Elvis fan," he says.

I thought he was the most charismatic person. Every time I saw him on a poster or in a store, I would just glare at it and say to myself—'Geez, do you think Elvis would ever come to this town? I wonder what he's doing now?'
I totally disagree with a lot of the things they say about Elvis. Being a performer, I know how it is, being married, to have women at your feet every night and then to go home. It's hard.

But does he think he's Elvis?

I was raised as a Jehovah's Witness. We believe that you don't go to heaven or hell. We believe there's a resurrection. Elvis will be resurrected among many other artists that got lost and didn't have a second chance. God knows that I'm putting a lot of happiness into people's hearts. They get a big thrill out of seeing me onstage. But, no, I don't ever think I'm Elvis.

Elvis has never communicated with Roi onstage, as he has with Wayne Newton, who told the *National Enquirer* in 1987 that Presley was speaking to him in the Las Vegas Hilton show room during his act.
"I don't do the pills," says Roi. "I have a few cocktails occasionally, and I'll smoke a cigarette sometimes, but that's it."
Roi says that Presley's image is still big in Vegas because "people don't want to let go of something that made them happy. Elvis made them feel good and high. Elvis was a glass of water on a hot day. And people want to hold on to that."

THE HIGH-WIRE ARTIST: JULIAN ALBULET

Every day when he goes to work, Julian Albulet climbs some sixty feet into the air and walks a tightrope across the mammoth Circus Circus casino with brother-in-law Mike Talamantez.
The Albulet Brothers are one of the sixteen acts that play daily at Circus Circus, giving families a place on the Strip to enjoy entertainment that isn't R-rated. And between acts, the family can enjoy the games of the midway. If the kids are old enough, they can patrol the midway by themselves, while mom and dad drop coin after coin in the one-armed bandits.
Doing a high-wire act is something of a thankless job, because the visitors, who tend to have kids in their arms, take the feat for granted. The crowds will look up for a few moments, and marvel at the two guys above them, then go about their business. For circus performers, working Circus Circus is the steadiest job in America. It means they can live in one town for an extended period of time. They can buy a home and raise a family, and the kids can go to the same school for a couple of years. No more all-night train rides and tutors.
The Albulet Brothers' high-wire show begins with the pair walking out onstage as the Circus Circus organist and drummer play "New York, New York" or the theme from "Hill Street Blues." They inch up a rope, arms outstretched, step into their booth in the air, and walk across the wire to the other side. En route, they jump over each other, stand on top of each other, hang from the rope by their hands, and then jump back on. Ten minutes later, they are across, and it's

applause time. The duo walks down the rope onto the ground, takes another bow, and heads back to the dressing room. The show is over. Next up: Charly Charles and his midget cycles.

"When I'm up there, I'm not thinking about the gamblers down there or the kids on the midway. I'm thinking about the trick and how it's supposed to be done," says Albulet.

> I do it in my mind before I do it. The tricks are the same, but the balancing is never the same. You have to balance every single time. It's like the Marines. It's not a job, it's an adventure.
>   You're challenging fate. As long as you know what you're doing, and don't go up there with a hangover, you'll be fine. It's like an airplane pilot bringing his plane into the airport. They don't think about falling or crashing, and neither do we.

Albulet has never fallen off the wire. He says he has no plans to. "You're safer up there than on the highway," he says. "Up there at least you're always aware of what's going on. There are more crazy people down there. You can get shot in a gang war or hit by a car. Up there it's just me and the wire."

Julian Albulet was born in Romania, where he worked for nine years in the Bucharest State Circus as an acrobat with "the Moshoianu Troupe," which featured eleven acrobats, all doing teeter-totters and somersaults. Ringling Brothers chiefs Irvin and Kenneth Feld saw them in Leningrad in 1968 and imported them for two seasons (1971–73). From there, Albulet worked two years in Germany, married circus showgirl Belinda, and returned to America in 1975.

The only job available with Ringling this time was as an electrician. He did that for a year, then quit, moved to Florida, and learned the art of high-wire performing. Since Florida is the circus capital of the world—and home base for Ringling—there were more than enough teachers nearby.

181

After a couple of years doing the act in small circuses all over the world, he heard of an opening in Reno at Circus Circus. He sent them a videotape of the act, together with some pictures, and was hired—more than happy to be settling down for a while. "Setting up for the circus is unbelievable work," he says. "To put up the wire takes so much time."

The Albulets moved to the much larger Circus Circus in Vegas in 1987. Julian and Belinda (a performer in the hotel's aerial ballet) live nearby with their two kids, Michael and Nadia, both of whom are learning gymnastics. A small wire for the kids to walk across runs the length of the living room in their house.

Albulet, whose impressive musculature is the result of backstage push-ups—an average of two hundred a day—works six days a week, usually from eleven to seven. "Once in a while, it really gets hard," he says.

You don't get too much time off. Okay, you really work only thirty minutes a day, but there's a mental stress that lasts *all* day. It's like twenty-four hours of pressure. You've got to be ready and on the ball. You can't relax up there. There is no second chance.

MAGIC

More magic is performed in Las Vegas than anywhere else in the world. Magicians in shows like *City Lites*, *Folies Bergère*, *Lido de Paris*, and *Abracadabra* and performers like David Copperfield (who plays eight weeks a year at Caesars) and Siegfried and Roy wow crowds each evening.

Vegas is a dream (get off the plane, invest a quarter, win a million), and magic appeals to all the dreamers who visit. It also appeals to the international audience. Gershwin tunes may sound familiar, but, to a foreigner, the lyrics can be hard to understand. What they *will* remember are those topless showgirls—and amazing tricks from the magician.

There are also more places to perform magic in Vegas than just about anywhere else. After all, there aren't a lot of revues in Cincinnati and Denver; magicians who play there have to put together an hour-long show. Vegas, of course, has a lot of revues, and each needs ten- to fifteen-minute magic acts. Show-room magic includes:

• Levitation: Siegfried and Roy, Melinda, Barclay Shaw, and Copperfield all make people and animals rise from the ground. Copperfield brings a woman onstage from the audience and levitates her. Siegfried levitates Roy and a tiger—together.

Magician David Copperfield out in the Vegas desert

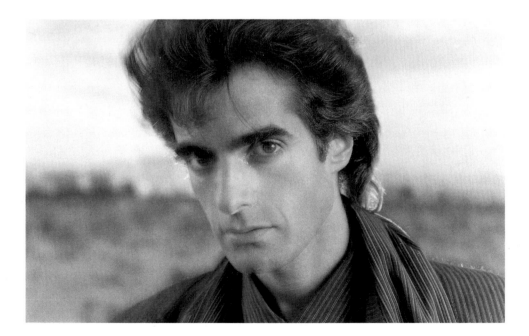

182

- The Transportation Trick: The lady gets in a box, a curtain quickly drops over it, and poof!—she is gone, an animal in her place.
- The Substitution Trunk: Harry Houdini's famous trick, in which a lady handcuffs the magician and puts him in a box, which is then tied up. A couple of seconds elapse and then poof!—the magician is on top of the box, unshackled. He opens the box and there's the lady inside, handcuffed.
- Disappearances: Roy rides a big gray elephant onstage and then poof!—he and the elephant are gone. Melinda drives a classic '60s yellow VW Beetle onstage to the tune of "California Girls." She steps out, waves her arm, and then poof!—it's gone. She also makes a boom box—poof!—disappear.
- The Vanishing Dove: Joseph Gabriel (*City Lites*), Lance Burton (*Folies Bergère*), Melinda, and Valentino (*Hot Lips*) wave their arms and poof!—white doves come flying out. They fly over the audience, return to the magician, and then turn into white silk hankies. Valentino goes one better. When he waves his arm, out comes a big duck.
- More Quackers: David Copperfield's co-star each evening is Webster the Duck, a little white animal who spends his off-hours relaxing in the Jacuzzi in his Caesars suite. During the Copperfield show, Webster does many tricks, including a duet with Consuelo the Chicken. The magician transforms Webster into a chicken and Consuelo into a duck. "Remember," warns Copperfield before the trick, "this is only an illusion." It sure looks weird.

David Copperfield's duck Webster, relaxing in the Jacuzzi at Caesars

"When we first started here, magic was always shoved at the back of the show," says Siegfried.

It never went on the marquee. Now almost every major show room has a magic act. Magic is in, now. In every one of us there's a child, and we all have dreams. You go to the movies today—which are the most popular? Steven Spielberg's fantasies. We fulfill those fantasies onstage. Las Vegas is a fantasy. It isn't reality. You can't compare it with any city in the world.

"I never was a magic fan," says *Splash* producer Jeff Kutash,

because I always thought that magic was set it up and knock 'em down—a con. You always knew going in that it was a trick, just like you knew that a comedian was going to give you a punchline. But I think that most audiences want to see something they haven't seen before. There's a whole new generation of people who haven't seen magic, and they enjoy it. And where else but in Vegas are they going to see it? Magic follows the Las Vegas guideline perfectly: Get the audience involved in the show.

Not only do magicians perform in virtually every show in town, but they also work the casino's restaurants and bars. Jimmy Grippo is the resident trickster at Caesar's Palace, Daniel Kros is at the Desert Inn, Michael Skinner at the Golden Nugget, and Dixie Dooley at the Holiday.

"At first, they didn't want magicians," says Grippo, who started at Caesars in 1968, "because they associated magicians with cheats. But I showed them that magicians are not cheaters. Cheating and magic don't go together. Cheaters can't do magic, and magicians can't cheat. They don't know how to cheat."

What Grippo and other hotel magicians specialize in is "close-up" magic, card and coin tricks performed at the table.

"Illusions are good," says Grippo, "but I'm interested in what the hand and the mind can do." Grippo's most popular illusion is "The Six Coins Trick." Grippo puts three coins in his left hand. Then he puts three coins in his right hand, along with a spectator's ring. He displays the three coins in the left hand and then the three coins and the ring in his right. The customer grabs both hands and says one, two, three. No coins in the left; six coins and the ring in the right.

One big Grippo fan was Jimmy Hoffa, the financier of Caesars.

Master close-up magician Jimmy
Grippo, who turned ninety in 1988,
doing a coin trick in front of Caesars
Palace

He loved the trick I did with the salt, where I put salt in my hand and it vanishes. Every
time he came to Vegas, he'd come with a group and have me do that trick for him.
He used to say to me, "I see how you could palm a card, but how can you palm
salt? There are so many particles."

Vegas entertainers are also big fans. At Grippo's big ninetieth birthday party at Caesars
in 1988, Frank Sinatra, Shirley MacLaine, Sammy Davis, Jr., George Burns, Tom Jones, and David
Copperfield were there on videotape to wish him many more years of success. "He's a living
legend," says Copperfield. "Anybody who knows anything about magic knows Jimmy Grippo."
"He's a great card manipulator," says Davis. "What's nice about Jimmy is he brings all of
the tricks down to the table level."
Grippo and the other hotel magicians work the various restaurants of their establishments,
walking up to the tables and booths to put a smile on people's faces while they eat. They
entertain high-rolling gamblers in their suites and near the gaming tables.
"I saw a guy one time take a table by himself and play baccarat," recalls Grippo.

He was playing $100,000 a hand. He lost $4,000,000 that day. He came upstairs
and had dinner. He was laughing, and he said, "Do some magic for me. Cheer me
up. I'm going to play again tomorrow. Maybe I'll get some luck." So I sit down and
do some magic. The next day he goes down, and he wins $6,000,000.

PART FOUR

THIS IS THE LIFE

CHAPTER 9
Working Vegas

It's the Capital of Craps, The Grand Boulevard of Chance, Moneytown, Bigtown, the Entertainment and Fun Capital of the World, the King of Cards, the Ruler of Roulette, the city where the doors never close.

Las Vegas, Las Vegas.

Where tourists visit but nobody lives. A city with no schools, markets, hospitals, or homes— just hotel rooms and all the shrimp cocktails you could ever want.

"People ask me where I live every day," says Dunes cocktail waitress Penny Munari. "When I tell them *here*, they say *where*? I tell them Las Vegas. They say, 'Yeah, but where?' They can't believe that anybody actually lives here. So I gave up. Now I tell them I commute."

When you live in a place known as "Sin City," people are naturally going to think that it is strange. Folks, after all, don't do a lot of gambling in Minnesota and Maine, and prostitution isn't legal in Nebraska and New Jersey. (Actually, it's legal only in Nevada counties that want it; Clark County, which encompasses Las Vegas, has outlawed the world's oldest profession. It is legal in nearby Pahrump, where there's a brothel by the side of the dusty dirt road. And if you don't want to make the one-hour drive, legend says you can always call the hotel bellhop and have him send up a pretty call girl. Visit any hotel lounge or walk down Las Vegas Boulevard—

Cocktail waitress Penny Munari

187

next to copies of the local and national newspapers are free pamphlets advertising the services of ladies of the night, with maps detailing routes to their establishments.)

In the blazing afternoon sun and the cool neon glow of the evening, Vegas is one of the most unusual cities in America. But the city with "Jackpot Lane," "Chance Avenue," and "Fortune Boulevard" was the first place comedian Pete Barbutti ever felt "normal."

"When you spend your entire life working with groups on the road, you're a misfit no matter where you go," says Barbutti, who came to Vegas from Scranton, Pennsylvania, in 1951.

You don't get to sleep till five A.M. and don't get out of the house until three in the afternoon. You get up and the post office, cleaners, and bank are closed, so you can't do anything. You go to a restaurant and get there at one in the afternoon, and the breakfast menu is off, so you have to get a hamburger.

When I moved to Vegas, I couldn't believe I was no longer a social freak. There were other people living the same hours, and nobody thought I was weird for ordering breakfast at three in the afternoon.

Living a normal life in Las Vegas is making sure that your non-working hours are spent west and east of Las Vegas Boulevard—in other words, off the Strip. Says veteran Vegas show producer Maynard Sloate (*Minsky's Burlesque; Norman, Is That You?*):

I've seen the sun rise over the desert many times. Before I got home. That was years ago, when I first got here. Now I never even drive down the Strip. Why would a local want to go near the Strip? There is a life and a way to live here off the Strip. We have beautiful homes, regular streets, we even have a freeway. If you live your life properly, you're not going to spend any time on the Strip, period. You are going to work on the Strip and spend the rest of your time elsewhere.

But for those who do spend time on the Strip, it can be tough. Vegas has a high suicide rate, attributable to the tough Vegas life-style.

"You can have a lot of problems here if you're a person who has addictions," says Caesars Palace cocktail waitress Sharon St. Clair. "Be it drinking, drugs, or gambling, if you're involved in any kind of habit, it's probably best not to come here. Like if you're a gambler, this is going to be a bad town to live in, for obvious reasons."

Ask anyone who works in Vegas—from Wayne Newton to the president of the Nevada division of Hilton; from the shift manager at the Frontier to cocktail waitress St. Clair—and they'll give you the standard refrain about gambling: You can't afford to live in Las Vegas and gamble. But everyone spends at least a little time at the tables when they first get here.

"There's no one in this town who has lived here and hasn't gambled," says Steve Poulos, a Stardust pit boss.

If you're going to go out and play the games, you'll go broke. You know what the best game to play is? Nothing. Even as a professional, I'm no better than anyone else. Being in the business, I might have a little edge since I know more about the games and the odds, but it still comes down to luck.

Roughly 65 percent of the workers in Vegas—the nation's seventieth largest city, with 660,000 residents—are employed by the hospitality trade. If they don't work at a casino, they work for companies involved with tourism in one way or another.

But there are also lots of shopping malls, grocery stores, schools, cleaners, and video stores (because of the late hours people work, more people own VCRs in Vegas than anywhere else in the continental United States). There are a few large non-gaming companies in town: Levi Strauss has a large jeans warehouse, taking advantage of the liberal Nevada tax policy, which doesn't include a storage tax; Ethel M. Chocolates, a subsidiary of M&M–Mars, makes liquor chocolates here, since Nevada is one of the few places in America where the manufacture

of alcoholic candy is legal; Nellis Air Force Base employs thousands, as do hospitals, law offices, auto garages, and other ordinary businesses found in Anytown, USA.

There are also stores that sell dice, gaming tables, and cards, dealer's uniforms, and antique slots. There is a course at the University of Nevada—Las Vegas on the "mathematics of casino games" (probabilities, expected values, rules, payoffs, and percentages of games), and there are more pawn shops per capita than anywhere else in the Union.

Real estate—purchase and rentals—is relatively inexpensive, food is cheap, everything's close by, and many stores are open twenty-four hours. Since real estate is affordable, most stores tend to be larger—rather than cramped, as in old urban areas like New York and Chicago. For Vegans, high on the list of activities away from the casinos is the university's star basketball team, the Runnin' Rebels. In the Entertainment Capital of the World, basketball is the hottest ticket in town.

Caesars cocktail waitress Sharon St. Clair, poolside

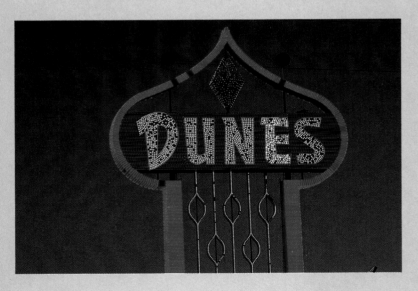

NEON

"Las Vegas," says Julio Iglesias, "is a strange city."

There isn't anything like Las Vegas anywhere but Las Vegas. It's a city of lights. I don't think there is anybody in the world who doesn't like the lights. In the morning, it's just dead in Vegas. At night the monsters wake up and everything is full of light again. It's much more brilliant, with the reflections of the lights, it makes people look like the front pages of magazines.

The sixteen million folks who visit Vegas each year can thank the Young Electric Sign Company for their red nighttime complexions. YESCO, as it is called, created, built, and services some 75 percent of the neon signs in town. That's virtually the entire downtown—the Horseshoe, the Mint, the Pioneer (home of neon cowboy Vegas Vic), the Fremont, and the Four Queens, along with the Strip classics—the Sahara, Circus Circus, the Sands, Bally's, and the Tropicana.

The concept of neon lighting was developed in the late nineteenth century by George Claude in Paris. Neon came to Vegas in 1946, when Ogden, Utah, sign maker Thomas Young—who had met with Claude in Paris in the 1920s—came south for a visit, trying to expand his business. He convinced the Boulder Club, an early downtown casino, that a giant light-studded marquee depicting Boulder Dam would boost biz. And the first Vegas neon sign was sold.

The club is no longer, and the dam is now called Hoover, but the era of megawatt signs is stronger than ever.

"The town was different then [in the 1940s]," says Young designer Rudi Crisostomo. "They had to have something. The flashing lights, the action, the animation. Once it got started, everybody started competing with each other to get the most tourists."

Young is based in Salt Lake, with offices in Idaho, Arizona, California, and Colorado (as well as Nevada); but 60 percent of the company's revenue comes from Vegas. Young's staffers sell, design, construct, and install new neon signs, which cost around $1,000,000 these days. They also service them, with a team that drives up and down the streets every night looking for blown bulbs. Young's army of forty bulb changers—who have twisted more than a quarter-million light bulbs and replaced more than three hundred miles of neon and fluorescent tubing over the years—returns in the A.M. to service the signs. Most times, they climb ladders mounted on trucks to get to the trouble spots. But some signs are so elaborate (like the Sahara's and the Mint's) that they're designed with an elevator inside for maintenance. (In the summer, the trick is to get to the signs between four-thirty and six-thirty A.M. When it's 100 degrees plus outside, it's only worse inside the neon sign.)

"The signs are like the lights that draw the moths," says YESCO art director Brian Leming. "The big hotels realize they have to spend the money to stay competitive. . . . The bigger and brighter the sign, the more people it attracts."

Vaughn Cannon, Jr., of the Young Electric Company, manufacturer of most Las Vegas neon

The neon graveyard at Young Electric

Young has built the tallest free standing sign—222 feet, 6 inches, for the Hotel Sahara—and a Strip masterpiece—the Circus Circus sign featuring "Las Vegas Lucky" the clown, the largest neon sign in terms of square footage. Vaughn Cannon, Jr., whose grandfather was Mr. Young himself, says Circus Circus is YESCO's greatest achievement. "Just think about it for a minute," he says. "You've got a 125-foot clown sitting up there in the air with a lollipop in his hand." (Young adds that one dark day Las Vegas Lucky required 1,300 new bulbs to be replaced.)

How does YESCO come up with new sign ideas?

Says Crisostomo:

A pizza maker wants his sign to look like a pizza; a plumber wants his sign to look like a monkey wrench. There are certain things you can do with a monkey wrench to make it look beautiful, but, if at all possible, we tell them to stay away from it. The expertise comes in how creative the designer is.

The more contemporary sign is much more difficult to design. You really need great shapes. Take the Flamingo sign. We lost that to another sign company, because when I was doing it, I was thinking of the bird itself, but the other designer, he was clever. He started the design from a feather, so it was simpler and more attractive. While I was using the whole bird, he was using a single feather.

"You have to have a wild imagination to come up with the 'Las Vegas look,'" says Leming. "The more you can do with lights—all the glitter and sparks you can get on it—that's what they're after."

Neon is actually less prevalent in Vegas than people think. Bally's sign has none—just white light and a purple plastic sheet with their name on it. Caesars has no neon on its marquee—just lightbulbs. Ditto for the Riviera, Frontier, and most of Circus Circus. "Yeah, I've seen those new signs," says Young neon blower Stan

Forrest. "Not a stick of neon on them, and they look like heck, don't they?"

What the resorts ask for these days are fields of reflector-backed light bulbs that dance, flicker, and seem to chase one another around in a swirl of light. Chasing lights are cheaper than neon to build and install, yet varied in their visual patterns and just as easy to maintain. Bulbs screw in and out and the sign does not have to be dismantled and trucked over to a specialist.

The other trend in new signs is the so-called message center—a sign within a sign, which flashes information about the hotel and casino. When cars get stuck in traffic jams on the Strip (which is often) folks can read the ads on the signs while waiting.

Signs. They are one of the hotel's most important investments. Rooms, pool, and lobby should look nice, but a great sign is going to be photographed by every tourist in town—as well as by the media. Says Cannon: "When the Sahara has the world's largest freestanding sign, they get national publicity for nothing."

The signs are small in Reno and Lake Tahoe, as are the resorts. In Atlantic City, the signs are larger, but, like topless showgirls, poker, and race and sports betting, neon has been outlawed there. "We're trying to create an effect that's reasonable and tasteful," Jay Fielder, city planner of Atlantic City, told the *New York Times* in 1985. "We'd rather have a cityscape dominated by architectural statements. Excessive signage effectively does nothing more than smudge that architecture."

The trend on the Strip may be for chasing light bulbs and message centers, but the one place neon junkies can still come for the greatest light show in the world is Fremont Street in downtown Las Vegas—a.k.a. Glitter Gulch.

There's one giant sign after the other: the bright turquoise of the Horsehoe, the orange orange of the Fremont; Vegas Vic, the neon cowboy, whose arm waves back and forth; Sassy Sally, the cowgirl across the street with the sexy neon gams. Imagine the surprise in neon heaven when Golden Nugget chairman

Steve Wynn took down his historic neon sign in 1984.

"Steve called me over and asked me what I thought, and I said, 'Steve, you're making a mistake,'" recalls Jack Binion of the Horseshoe Club, Wynn's neighbor across the street. "That was one of the most photographed signs in the world."

"I got burned out on that goddamned neon and said, 'This is ugly. I don't care if it's distinctive, it's ugly, and I can't stand ugly." says Wynn. "All of these signs are particularly ugly in the daytime. They don't work. Even if you turn them on, they look ridiculous."

When Wynn decided to transform the Nugget from a middle-market establishment to a classy, high-roller haven, he decided he could do not only without a neon sign, but without any sign at all—something unheard of in Vegas.

"We realized that anything they did across the street would be reflected at night on our white marble," Wynn says.

I wanted to put up something that could capture daytime brightness and animation. I put as many bulbs back on our marble as there were in the sign. We were doing the same thing, only we were doing it better. Instead of just blasting ugly bulbs, mounted on painted metal, we put some design up there.

Obviously, Wynn's bold stand didn't sit too well with those in the neon community.

"In this town, you either like it or you don't," says Vaughn Cannon, Jr. "The consensus of the people that I talk to is that it doesn't belong downtown. I agree."

Tom Wolfe once wrote that Vegas was a unique city in that there was no skyline—just a signline. I think he's wrong. When you drive or fly into Vegas, the first thing you see is a hotel-line, with a purple glow emanating from the stretch of neon.

If New York is historic buildings, Las Vegas is hotels and signs. That's it.

When people come to visit, they don't go to see a landmark like the Empire State Building; they flock to ornate gambling halls like Caesars Palace and Circus Circus. Then it's on to the downtown neon of Glitter Gulch, followed by Hoover Dam and Wedding Chapel Row.

A lot of people say there's nothing to do in Las Vegas but gamble. That's not true. Vegas now has a water park and a museum of natural history on the Strip, a zoo, and the Liberace Museum. Get off the Strip, and Vegas seems like any booming desert city—like Phoenix or Palm Springs.

Besides the neon and gaudiness of some of the stranger attractions, what's really weird about the Strip is that there are no places to buy food. If you want a snack, you're forced to select hot dogs and Fig Newtons or else eat at a coffee shop. There is no 7-Eleven—no market of any kind. It's hotel/casinos only, and just try buying an apple or orange from one of *them*.

Nevertheless, you *will* find lots of "juice" on the Strip. Want a good seat in a show room? Give the maître d' a little juice in the form of a "toke." Winning at blackjack? It's local custom to juice the dealer with a toke. Does toking the dealer help you win? Not at all; it's just a custom, like giving a tip to a waitress in a restaurant.

There are two reasons the Vegas hotel/casino industry makes a fortune ($8,600,000,000 in 1987). First of all, there's the fact that guests freely decide to hand over millions of dollars on the gaming tables and slots; secondly, most employees work for minimum wage. They make their money via the toke, or the tip. No one can come to Vegas and escape the juice.

Take an imaginary airplane ride here and you'll see. Get off the plane and hail a cab to the hotel. Tip #1 goes to the driver. Check in at the hotel and have your bags brought up to the room. There goes tip #2. Take a swim at the pool and get a towel from the attendant. That's tip #3.

Go back to the room, change, and go out for dinner. The maître d' gets a tip for a good table, the waiter gets a tip for the service. That's #4 and #5.

Visit a wedding chapel and get married after dinner, pay the chapel fee and then give a "donation" to the minister. Tip #6.

Take in a show afterwards, and the maître d' there gets a tip for a good table, as does the captain. And then, of course, the waiter who serves the drinks. #7, #8, #9.

Play some table games after the show, win some money, and the dealer is going to be expecting his toke. Tip #10. And so it goes.

THE WEDDING WARS

Hollywood made Vegas. The movie stars who came to this nearby desert community for some gambling and relaxation enticed the rest of the nation to discover the playland of the stars. They also discovered that the stars were doing more than just gambling—they were also getting married and divorced.

The famous "wide open" gambling bill that was signed in 1931 also included provisions liberalizing marriage and divorce laws. Six weeks' residency was required for a divorce; no blood test or waiting for a wedding—all you needed was a license and some money.

At first, Reno, with its dude ranches, was where most people went to get divorced. In the 1950s, El Rancho Vegas and the Last Frontier tried to cater to the women as well, encouraging them to spend six fun weeks in the Vegas sun waiting for their residency papers. The hotels didn't do a lot of business, however. Reno was for divorces, Vegas was for weddings—especially those involving Hollywood stars, such as Mickey Rooney and Elaine Mahnken (1952); Joan Crawford and A. N. Steele (1955); Steve and Eydie (1957); Paul Newman and Joanne Woodward (1958); Sammy Davis, Jr., and Loray White (1958); Mary Tyler Moore and Grant Tinker (1962); Elvis and Priscilla (1967); Joan Collins and Peter Holm (1985).

In 1954 the Las Vegas Chamber of Commerce announced that marriages had exceeded

The Elvis-Priscilla nuptials

divorces that year six to one. Hollywood weddings, Vegas-style, were news events. Stars would time their weddings for slow or big news days. Stripper Lili St. Cyr postponed her marriage to Ted Jordan three times so it would coincide with the atom blast of February 21, 1955, and both the blast and her wedding shot would be in the papers.

It's still big news when stars run to Vegas for a quickie wedding. But stars aren't the only ones getting betrothed in the wedding capital of the world, where about 70,000 weddings are performed each year in twenty-five-plus chapels. (Valentine's Day and New Year's Eve are the two biggest days.)

"I've done more weddings here in eight months," says Rev. Verne Curry, a minister at the Circus Circus wedding chapel, "than I did in thirty-eight years working at parishes in New

Hampshire, Maine, and Illinois. Getting married in Vegas is like going to Niagara Falls for a honeymoon. It's just the thing to do."

"Let's face it, this is a business," says Dr. John P. Levendis, a Candlelight Wedding Chapel minister.

> Back home you can have the wedding with all the fuss and expense and spend $10,000. Or you can come to Las Vegas, get your marriage license, and get the same ceremony, in essence, for much less. A complete wedding, if it were done in a church with a minister, a choir, and organist, would cost $10,000 to $15,000.

At the Candlelight, the marriage ceremony is served à la carte. The basic charge is $45 to use the chapel, $27 for the wedding license, $75 for the video, and $15 to $129 for pictures. Want some music? For $10, they'll slip a cassette tape of "Here Comes the Bride" into the tape deck. For $25 the organist will perform it live.

Newlyweds-to-be wait in line outside the chapel (sometimes as long as an hour, if business is backed up on a busy Saturday). Inside, the chapel looks just like a church, with rows and rows of pews. Walk down the aisle, and the minister (or a rabbi for Jewish couples) greets candidates with "You're now in the sight of God," etc., leading up to "Do you take this woman to be your lawfully wedded wife . . . " and the instruction to the couple to kiss. "Now sit and look lovingly in each other's eyes while I prepare the wedding certificate."

The photographer walks up to the couple and hands them an envelope, saying that the minister is not paid by the chapel, and that a minimum donation of $25 or more is suggested.

On two Saturdays that I spent at the Candlelight, Dr. Levendis performed fifty weddings, as his wife sat next to him counting the profits for the day. "Everyone thinks ministers make so much money here, but they really don't," she told me, holding a giant wad of green bills as she spoke. "We have to give the chapel $6 for every wedding performed."

So, okay, instead of $1,250 for the day, they'll walk away with $950. Still not too bad for a day's work.

After managing chapels on and off for some thirty years, Charlotte Richards became a minister herself in 1985 because she wasn't happy with the way weddings were being presented.

Vegas wedding mogul Charlotte Richards, owner of four Vegas wedding chapels, including the Little White and We've Only Just Begun

"I saw so many ministers that worked for me that were doing fast-food 'doyoutakethiswoman-tobeyourwife? doyoutakethismantobeyourhusband? Okay, Inowpronounceyoumanandwife.' It was just crude. People would say, 'Is that all there is?' I couldn't see a happy starting point there. I felt I had something to offer them, some love and some feeling and some experience."

Richards came to Vegas from Oregon in 1957 with her three young kids and her husband of six years, only to have her husband leave her soon after she arrived. She fell in love with the owner of her apartment building, Merle Richards, and married him. Richards was also owner of the Little Church of the West, the historic first chapel in Vegas. At the time they wed (in Reno, of all places) the church was on the property of the Last Frontier Hotel, on the Strip. Today, it's been moved—physically—down to the Hacienda.

She and Richards ran the chapel and eventually opened another on the Strip, the Candlelight. But their own marriage ran into trouble when Merle Richards started drinking heavily. One night, drunk, he sold the Candlelight for a measly $5,000.

Charlotte Richards tried to fight the sale in court, but got nowhere. Depressed, she moped around the chapel, dreading the day they had to give it up to the new owners. One day, down as low as she could get, she stood in the doorway of the chapel, crying. A man across the street saw her and came to console her. Richards told him her life was over, that she no longer had any reason to live. "He prayed for me, and told me that Jesus loved me." As he told her more about Christ, she decided to "give my life to God"—and leave her husband.

"We had everything," she says, "but I figured I'd rather have peace with God than die a slow death of alcoholism."

After four years of traveling across the country, telling anyone who would listen about "the goodness of Jesus," she returned to Vegas following the death of an aunt, who left her a pile of money—enough to enter the wedding business again. It didn't take off until the day a big TV star walked through her doors.

"Those are the little favors that God does for you. We were doing something like a hundred weddings a month; immediately it shot up to four hundred a month."

Joan Collins chose Richards's Little White Chapel for her wedding day. Richards put up a sign: "Dynasty's Joan Collins was married here." The wedding got a big write-up in the *National Enquirer* and the *Star*.

A little less than a year later, Collins and hubby Peter Holm were involved in a very nasty divorce, but that didn't stop the Little White from continuing to offer the "Joan Collins special," a $500 wedding that includes live organ music, champagne, wedding cake, wedding certificate holder, garter, limo, and nineteen photographs.

"I was really hurt when I heard about the divorce," says Richards. "I thought, shame on that Peter Holm. What a bad boy. But I don't like to see anybody get divorced. I wish there could have been some way to help them."

Wedding Row on Las Vegas Boulevard South begins at the Sahara and continues downtown. Once the busy intersection is crossed, the chapels pop up with their neon signs among the McDonalds, adult book shops, 7-Elevens, and tiny motels.

You can get married anywhere you want in Las Vegas. Richards will come to your hotel room. Or your car. The basket of a hot-air balloon. A mountaintop. She'll perform the ceremony from the front seat of her silver Rolls Royce, as the couple sits in the back seat. You can get married in a chapel anytime you want—most are open twenty-four hours. If they're not, they'll open the place for you, say if you want to get married at two A.M.

The name of the game in the Chapel Biz is selling hard on the telephone. That's when the best pitch must be made, since rates tend to be about the same all over town.

The pitch is love. Richards's phone number for the Little White is 1-800-364-LOVE. Her telephone has "I love you" written in white and pink letters with heart signs all over the cord.

"Being remarried helps me considerably to be a minister," she says, "because every time I say a marriage vow, I think about my marriage."

"You will get a few people that think this is a joke," says Marianne Cantino, manager of the Circus Circus chapel.

"Do people really get married like this?" Most of these people are from back East, and they usually get married in a church and have one of those big weddings. They just can't understand that people would just take off and get married with no families or whatever. But the people from California and Arizona—they think this is just great.

Well, not everybody. Gordon Gust, owner of the Candlelight, Wee Kirk O' the Heather, and Little Church of the West, says he gets many calls the next day asking for an annulment.

They say, "This isn't what I thought it was going to be." But we can't do that. Once they take their vows, the minister has to turn in the license and abide by the laws of the state, which is that if they want to come here and be a resident, six weeks later their marriage can be annulled.

One early morning at the Candlelight, a couple came in and decided to get married at sunup.

They had met three hours earlier at the Peppermill [cocktail lounge] . . . had never known each other before, but they decided to get married. She kept saying, "Do you believe what I'm doing? I can't." We said, "Why are you doing this?" and she said that she just knew this was the guy for her. Four years later they came back to visit with another couple from Michigan—which is where they live—along with a beautiful two-year-old daughter.

THE BEST JOB IN VEGAS

The ultimate Vegas jackpot isn't winning the Million Dollar Pot O' Gold slot at the Hilton; it's being hired as maître d' in a hot hotel show room. It's better than being a hotel president, better than a casino manager. Carrying a $250,000- to $300,000-a-year stipend, its only drawback is that you work six nights a week from six P.M. to two A.M.

"If I had to do it all over again, and could choose any job in Vegas, it would be maître d', no question about it," says Bill DeAngelis, former entertainment director and executive producer for the MGM Grand.

Making $5,000 or $6,000 a week is nothing. Tax free. Cash. Wouldn't you love to go to work every night not knowing how much you were going to make? Whether you were going to top $1,000 or $2,000? You could have a $10,000 night. I used to walk in their count room while the show was going on . . . if you could have seen that table . . . it looked like a garden of lettuce, black chips, $25 chips, $5 chips, $100 bills. Unbelievable. More money than you've ever seen in your life.

Sounds great, doesn't it? Don't bother applying. It is virtually impossible to get hired for the job. Once they board the gravy train, Angelo, Bobby, Howie, Court, Rudy, Johnny, and Sven (to name a few of the town's maître d's) don't want to give it up.

How do they make so much money? Simple. The hotel's best gamblers are regularly given free "duckets" (comps) to the show room. Big gamblers, who tend also to have big egos, never want to sit with the peons at a table. They want a booth, and there are usually only about forty in a show room. Tipping to get a booth is nothing when you've been given free seats to the show. The average tip is between $100 and $200, and there's forty booths. Which means it's theoretically possible to score $8,000 to $16,000 *a night* for two shows a night.

Naturally, the maître d's claim the stories of their enormous winnings are greatly exaggerated. "Yes, you make great money," says Emelio Muscelli, the former maître d' of the Las Vegas Hilton.

But don't forget, we have to split it with twenty-two captains [and the other employees of the show room]. Don't forget that the show room exists solely to bring people in to gamble in the casino. A lot of people think the maître d' is in business for himself. It's a balancing act—I'm not going to sell a seat to a customer when the casino expects me to hold the seat for a *casino* customer.

The system at the Hilton, as well as every other casino, gives preferred seating—and comps—to the gamblers, while non-gamblers must wait in line. Hypothetically, you could wait in line all day and find a gambler waltzing in right in front of you.

"I have to hold the best seats for them," says Caesars Palace maître d' Angelo Giouzelis.

It all depends on the action of the casino how many I'll be holding. I also hold seats for hotel guests. I think if they're staying here and spending money here, they should have preference over the guy who walks in off the street.

Wedded bliss, Vegas-style

Angelo Giouzelis has the greatest job in Vegas: show room maitre'd.

Giouzelis is different from his colleagues in that he publicly states that he can't be bought.

I won't accept a tip, and I'm bragging about it. Why do I feel that way? The customer shouldn't have to have his hand in his pocket all night, tipping me and the captain and the waiter, spending money right and left.

But don't think that means Giouzelis isn't going to walk away with a bundle. As maître d', he still splits the tips fifty-fifty with the captains of the show rooms—they are the guys who show people to their seats.

People think the maître d' is a guy who stands there, looks good, and makes a ton of money every night. Not true. You've got to have a big belly, throw all the things inside, and never take it home, because this job is about pressure.

What pressure? During the glory days of the Rat Pack at the Sands, Muscelli served as maître d' for a show room that sat only five hundred. "Sometimes the percentage of casino customers that wanted to see the show was 95 percent," he says. "I could have sold five thousand tickets if I had wanted to."

"You wonder why I talk about the knot in my stomach?" asks Giouzelis.

How about the time a blind man on New Year's Eve refused to pay because he said he couldn't see the show? Or the time a woman said, "I refuse to sit next to that couple" because she didn't like the way they were dressed? Or the guy who excused himself to go to the bathroom so that he didn't have to pay the check?

People continually take shots at you. You've got to smile, be quick, make decisions, and be gracious. Here you have to deal with a guy that's been gambling in the casino, he loses a great sum of money and he is going to be upset and ready to argue. You have to learn to live with it.

CHUCK

Another day at the world-famous Circus Circus $3.98 dinner buffet, home of forty-five different mouth-watering selections. The line extends from the front door down to the wedding chapel near the gift shop, as the tourists (some 10,900 a day) are about to eat all they want. The patrons are eager with excitement, knowing that inside the big pink room specials await like Sausage Portuguese, Salisbury Steak, chicken fritters, mashed potatoes, ravioli and meatballs, red and green Jell-o, and egg rolls. And then there's an after-dinner treat, what many consider the finest delicacy known to civilization—frozen dairy dessert.

It's the Vegas buffet, that strange never-never land where Chef Boy-ar-dee, Mr. Swanson, and Mrs. Paul all seem to have collaborated on the ultimate TV-dinner. It's not a world that Circus Circus has unto itself. Like macaroni and cheese and fish sticks? They are part of the package at the Sahara's $5.55 "Garden Buffet." Baked pollack, cauliflower au gratin, and potato leek soup are just some of the goodies available at the Riviera's $4.95 "gourmet" buffet.

And if you like shrimp cocktail, why, you can get that at every buffet in town.

In the beginning, the buffet was known simply as chuck: The Las Vegas Chuckwagon, where you could eat like a king—in limitless portions—for a low price. Good Chuck. All night long.

Vegas and food have always had a very special relationship. It is a good draw to get gamblers into the casino. There's chuck for the players, the coffee shop for blackjackers, and then the "gourmet rooms" for the high rollers.

The Sultan's Table, the gourmet room at the Dunes, was the first such establishment in town. It began in 1961, after Dunes owner Major Riddle went to Mexico City and saw a restaurant with a similar theme. He enjoyed the atmosphere, thought it would be right for Vegas, and hired Clement Lopez and his Magic Violins to play in the room.

The Sultan was the original mascot of the Dunes, a thirty-foot turban-topped man who used to live above the Dunes's front entrance. He is long gone, but his table is still in the casino, an "epicurean adventure" that costs around $100 for two (plus tip for the fiddlers, who still play every night for your dining pleasure). The Sultan's Table serves lots of meats—chow like calves' sweetbreads and rack of lamb.

At the other gourmet room of the Dunes, the Dome of the Sea, a live mermaid (with fins) replaces the fiddlers; she plays the harp while patrons munch on frog legs, Shrimp Christina, and Boston Bibb lettuce.

At the Caesars Palace gourmet room, the gals are called Wine Goddesses and look a lot like the Dunes mermaid, except they have full use of their feet. The goddesses of the Bacchanal Room wear diaphanous, Middle Eastern two-piece costumes, and they don't play the harp. They pour the wine, serve grapes, and give back rubs to the gentlemen before coffee is served. The six-course Roman feast with three dinner wines is served without a menu—just a $110 bill for two, plus tips for the waiter, maître d', and captain. Typical meal: Proscuitto with melon as the appetizer, hot sorrel soup, Salmon Veronique, salad with tomatoes and artichoke hearts, Chicken Angelo, Veal Oscar or Tournedos Rossini, vanilla ice cream with fruit, chocolates and other sweets, and coffee.

The restaurants at the Las Vegas Hilton are in step with the rest of the Hilton chain. No fancy dress, no back rubs, and no mermaids. What the Vegas Hilton has is more restaurants—fourteen of 'em—and they're not done in shopping-mall food-court style. They run the gamut from Chinese, to chops, to Italian, to French.

"We serve 16,000 meals a day here at our fourteen restaurants," says Hilton food and beverage vice president Paul Houdayer. "We have to have variety. We want to serve our customers and make sure they stay in our hotel. Because if they stay in our hotel, then we have a chance for them to visit our casino, and then we have a chance to win some money."

Heyday of the Las Vegas Chuck-wagon—home of "Good Chuck"

201

Houdayer says the Las Vegas Hilton grosses more food and beverage dollars than any other Hilton hotel—$66,000,000 a year. And the hotel also orders an incredible amount of food each year. Like 2,500,000 eggs, 78,000 pounds of bacon, 60,000 pounds of strip sirloin, 28,000 gallons of orange juice, 250,000 heads of lettuce, and 58,000 pounds of bean sprouts.

COCKTAILS

Next time you walk through a casino, listen for the sound of clickers. That's the pit boss signaling to the cocktail waitress that it is time to get some drinks to a gambler at a table. Traditionally, when a gambler is winning, the pit boss moves some alcohol into his blood to dull the brain.

In the casino, odds are you'll see more dealers and cocktail waitresses than any other employees. Most dealers look the same—they wear either bow ties or nice shirts or western garb. But the cocktail waitresses are another story. Low-cut dresses and cleavage a-plenty,

Cocktail waitresses—Robin Pullen of the Stardust and (opposite) Sandy Magg of the Las Vegas Hilton

chorus-girl tights, mini-skirts, Roman garb, western dress, Arabian costume—you name it. One thing is constant: They've got to be pretty, have nice legs, and be able to fend off the sexual advances of drunken gamblers all night long.

And the uniform has got to be flashy. "What would you think if a cocktail waitress came up to you in black slacks and a white shirt?" asks Gary Sawina, the man at the Hotel Sahara in charge of deciding what the cocktail waitresses should wear. "You would feel like you were out of place. This is Vegas, after all."

Cocktails is one of the great Vegas gigs. Waitresses don't have to collect bills. Anyone playing games in the casino—from nickel slots to $100,000-a-hand baccarat—qualifies for free drinks. In return, players are expected to show their appreciation by tipping the waitress. That's usually no problem, because most people have either a bucket of coins by their side or some chips. But, let's face it, not everyone feels generous.

"I try to be nice to them," says Stardust cocktail waitress Robin Pullen. "Sooner or later, I figure they'll give me a tip. It's like a challenge if they don't. You keep working on them until they do. It's like, how many drinks do I have to bring until they'll give me a tip?"

Pullen works the Stardust, a casino considered a "grind joint," meaning that the low rollers play there. But what's it like to serve cocktails to high rollers in the grand baccarat pit at Caesars, where more money can be dropped in one day than in some entire casinos?

Such is the life of Sharon St. Clair, a former Australian acrobat who moved to Vegas as a teenager in the 1960s.

"When I first started working in the baccarat pit, I used to get so absorbed by it that I would get too involved for my own good," she says. "I used to think, 'Oh, my God, I could buy a house with that.' But you learn after a while that you have to separate yourself from that. It's not realistic. You just have to serve the drink and be amused by the carryings on."

Of course, she will admit that an occasional "big score" can happen on her shift, but the days of the $500 and $1,000 tips are few and far between. Most of the time, she says, it's a $5 tip—which ain't too bad.

St. Clair came to Vegas as part of an act that played the *Casino de Paris* at the Dunes Hotel for seven years. When the show closed, "I decided that was enough of applause; now I wanted to make some real money." She thought cocktails would be "exciting and glamorous." Caesars cocktail waitresses are called "goddesses," they wear short uniforms accentuating the bust, and the hairdo has got to be seen to be believed. "This is all wig," says St. Clair.

The hairdresser here puts it on for us. Basically, our hair is pulled up in a knot. This thing is hollow, so we can put our hair there and away we go. We come to work in the morning and pick up our heads. Our hair stays here every day, along with our uniforms. It's like show biz. We have our own dressing rooms.

At the Stardust, there isn't much of a decision about what to do with the hair. It either goes up or down. The question is whether or not to spice up the cleavage. "They don't ask us to do anything," says Pullen. "We wear the uniform they provide us with. I don't have mine cut down, but a lot of the girls do. Some of the girls cut them shorter. I don't have a lot of cleavage anyhow. When I worked at Circus Circus, they gave us pillows to put in our cleavage."

The cocktails contingent gets to hear every line in the book.
"How did your legs get so shiny?"
"How far up do your legs go?"
"What's a good place to go to dinner?" Hugo's. "Will you come with me?"
Dunes cocktail waitress Penny Munari says she just laughs and walks away when such lines are trotted out, and she tells people she's married (which is true). But getting hit on is a hazard of any job in which a woman wears skimpy outfits. Over the years Munari has worn a purple polyester penguin suit with white top hat, a black-and-white vestlike top with bikini bottom, and—currently—an Arabian-styled black outfit with swimsuit underneath and veils over her legs and arms.

203

Kyong Huff is a Caesars "wine goddess," who pours vino and offers massage to gentlemen customers in the Bacchanal Room.

"Wearing the costumes felt strange at first," she says, especially some of the scantier ones. But I got used to it."

A lot of girls go into the job looking to meet somebody. One girl had a teaching credential, but her goal was to meet somebody—and she did. They set goals of coming in, meeting somebody, and then getting out. I've never looked at it that way. I'm there to make money. The harder I work at the job, the more money I'll make. If I was a secretary and busted my ass typing and filing, my boss isn't going to reward me with extra money, but if I hustle with cocktails here I will definitely make more money.

A former stripper from Detroit ("I wasn't nasty, I was just dancing and having a good time doing it"), Robin Pullen decided to hang up the pasties and leave for Vegas in 1970, after visiting on a vacation. She quit her secretarial day job back home, pulled her two sons out of school, and headed west, where she was working within the first three days.

Her first job was as a waitress at the El Cortez Hotel's coffee shop. "I kept asking the bar manager to put me in cocktails," she says. "The money's better, and you just go to the bar and pick up your drinks and serve them. When you serve food, you've got to go back and pick up the toast; you gotta get the juice. You make so many trips before you finally get your check."

Working the graveyard shift, Pullen met her second husband, a slot-machine mechanic. They love working the two A.M. to ten A.M. shift. "You have your days free to do other things. You can do the same thing in the day that others do at night: go out to dinner, to a movie, bowling, skiing—everything."

After leaving work, she stays up all day, goes to bed at five P.M., and awakes at midnight. She eats dinner with her husband at two in the afternoon.

"Lost Wages. What a great play on words."

—Milton Berle

Sharon St. Clair

St. Clair works the twelve P.M. to eight P.M. shift, a relatively quiet time in the casino. She chose "day" since she takes classes at the university and has a side business as a travel agent. "Cocktails enables me to travel and see a lot of the world," she says.

It's easy living. I don't think I could live this kind of life in Australia. I couldn't do three things at the same time. The opportunities are less, you couldn't work in cocktails and make as much as I do, the cost of living is higher. I've achieved a great deal for someone who was a foreigner and came here with nothing.

BAGS

A hotel is a hotel is a hotel, but Caesars Palace is different. Giant fountains splash water in front, a blue glow emanates from each room window, the cocktail lounge is a barge with a nude Cleopatra on the bow, cocktail waitresses have those strange hairdos—and then there's Joey, the singing bellman.

Joey Ciadella wheels bags down the marble corridors of the Palace crooning Mario Lanza tunes and "You've Got to Have Heart" from *Damn Yankees*. (The key line of the song is "When your luck is batting zero, get your chin up off the floor.")

"People come to Las Vegas, I don't care what town they come from, they want to forget their little problems," he says. "When you're singing to them and relate to them, they respond."

With the shift in emphasis in Vegas from a high-roller haven to a home for the masses, local bellhops complain their business has gone way down. Folks from Ohio and Kansas don't want their bags carried for them, and now that AIDS is a concern, bellmen can't even arrange any call-girl side business, which used to be a staple of the Vegas bellman.

Joey Ciadella, the singing bellman
of Caesars Palace

But times are still good at Caesars, where most rooms start at $100, and big gamblers still like to have their bags brought up for them.

"You make a living, you make a good living," says Ciadella.

You've got to take care of the people and build up a rapport with them, because anybody can take bags and put them in a room. What I do is go to the room, open the door . . . SHOW them the fire escape. SHOW them how the shower works. HOW to turn on the TV. HANG their hanging bags—don't just throw them in the room— HANG THEM. Ask if I can unpack them. Nine out of ten will say no, but once in a while you run into a guy who wants to go down and do his thing right away, and he'll say, "Joey, take care of it for me." That's where they get to know you.
Service. We're a service-oriented business. You've got to take care of the people.

And what brought the singing bellhop to Vegas? Misfortune. He had been running a thriving motel in the New York suburbs, which he had to give up when the New York State Thruway decided to build an off-ramp over his property. He packed his bags in 1966 and gave Vegas a try. "I figured it would be a progressive town." Ciadella quickly got a job as a waiter at the Mint Hotel, but just as quickly left for a lower-ranked job—as busboy at the Caesars Palace coffee shop. "It was a step down, but I figured Caesars would be a progressive place. Being Italian, I figured I'd blend right in."
He did. Progressively. Within a couple of years he was promoted to waiter, then captain of the ritzy Bacchanal Room, the most expensive joint in the house.
But Ciadella longed for bags. He asked to be switched over because it's "closer to the people. I like relating to people on a one-to-one basis. In my business it's all presentation and service. You explain all the facilities and amenities you have here, and then you leave and hope you build up a rapport with them."

The tips are what enticed Torch Alstaugh, a long-time bellman at the Tropicana, to get into the business. "I'd see these people making these huge tips, and I said, 'Damn, they're making lots of money. That's the business for me.'"

206

But Alstaugh says the days of the great tips are over.

Let me tell you, the tipping employee is the most forgotten employee of all service industries. The tips have not increased in over thirty years. I make as much in tips today as I did back then. People are tipping the same—when the cowboys were here for the rodeo, they were just the worst. I carried sixteen bags for one of them, and all I got was a dollar. And I had to lug those bags all the way through the casino.

Alstaugh grew up in Vegas, joined the military, and then decided to get into the casino business. Like Ciadella, he started in the restaurant end of things, but then he asked for bags.

What really got me was that, as a waiter, you have a whole station to deal with, and you can have sometimes twenty or thirty people in your station, and they're all like, "Where's this?" "Where's that?" and, after a while, it gets to you. It's the toughest job in the world.
     Bags are a lot more physical, but they're also easier because you're dealing with people one-on-one. Anytime you deal with people one-on-one it's much better, and you make more money than a waiter.

The bellman has a special place in Vegas history because he was traditionally responsible for securing ladies of the evening. All the visitor had to do was casually ask the bellman to send someone up, slip him $20, and await the knock on his door.
     These days, says Ciadella,

as soon as they mention anything about sex, I tell them they better go buy a whole rubber suit and cover their whole body, because once you indulge, you're a goner. With AIDS you hardly even see the hookers around here anymore. Ten years ago they were all over the place, in lounges, in the lobbies, all over. They were flagging down customers on the street. But not anymore.

PHONES

"Paging Clyde Shitface. Phone call for Clyde Shitface." Little games like that are played every day in the Vegas casinos, where adults in a party mood have fun asking the phone operators to page people with X-rated names.
     Unlike office buildings, where folks are often "away from their desk" or "in a meeting," most people can actually be found in the casinos. They'll be able to hear the operator calling out their names in the casino, on the elevator, on hotel floors, in the coffee shop—just about everywhere. To make doubly sure, most casino executives walk around with beepers attached to their belts. When they leave the casino, many carry portable cellular telephones, which enable them to take calls on the streets, in cars, at restaurants, anywhere. Vegas isn't just the entertainment, wedding, neon, and fun capital of the world, it's also the portable cellular capital. And not just for casino executives: minister Charlotte Richards brings her cellular with her everywhere she goes. The night Bruce Willis was looking for a minister to marry him and Demi Moore, Golden Nugget owner Steve Wynn found Richards at a restaurant. She left her food, got in her car, and drove down to the Nugget. She has also been known to take calls at the supermarket, her doctor's office, and in elevators.
     But most cellular sales are to casino officials. It is the hotel switchboard operator's job to connect callers to the cellulars or home numbers. The operator also screens calls for celebrities.
     What a job, being a switchboard operator at a Vegas hotel! Here you've got the five largest hotels in America (with around 3,000 rooms each) and a whole lot of calls coming in. The Las Vegas Hilton places some 30,000 a day through its switchboard; Bally's does 25,000— and their operators have to conclude each conversation with "Have a lucky day!"
     "We have forty operators here," says Bally's telecommunications manager Mary Ward. "In

The PBX room at Caesars

a hotel this size our main business is conventions. The delegates are usually up in the morning, and they hit us hard for two or three hours, then they go and do their business, come back, and hit us hard again in the evening."

In the PBX rooms, two rows of switchboard operators sit by their telephones and computers. They use the computer screen to find the room number of the guest who is being called. On the wall is a blackboard with special instructions: whose calls should be screened, which executives have beepers, and which ones want calls transferred to the cellular.

"We talk to all types here," says Hilton PBX operator Dottie Reed, "people from all walks of life, people of every nationality. Sometimes you're a babysitter for kids and adults. We talk to husbands all the time who have lost their wives in the casino. We have to tell them where to go, and we page their wives."

While it can be a madhouse down in the casino on Saturday nights, it can be total mania in the PBX room during a special event. Once, during a big boxing match, some 58,000 calls came in to the Hilton during a twenty-four-hour period. "It was just crazy," says Reed. "It got so I lost my voice completely at the end of the day. The last thing I wanted to hear when I got home was the phone ringing."

During those crazy periods, Ward, who began as an operator at the Flamingo in the 1950s, will pick up the phone herself and help out.

"I love the feeling of being able to connect the calls through where they're supposed to go," she says. "No matter how fancy the equipment gets, the operator is always [needed], because you need that personal touch with the customer."

ROOM SERVICE WAITER

Answering the phone at a giant hotel may be a lot of work, but at least you can sit while you do it. A position as room service waiter at one of the five biggest hotels in America is a job with lots of exercise. "On a slow day," says André Beaudry, a room service waiter at the 3,200-room Las Vegas Hilton, "I'll walk ten miles. On a busy day I'll do twenty."

Riviera room service waiter Willie Rodriguez delivering his goods

208

The entire Hilton is a quarter-mile from one end to the other—the size of a football field. Beaudry says he can cover it within five minutes. The room service process begins with the phone call from the room; the order is brought to the kitchen, and food is ready in about twenty minutes. It is then given to the waiter, who brings it upstairs. "I can get up there in about five minutes, if the elevator is in my favor," he says. There are nine service elevators.

"It's not unusual for us to serve 1,500 meals a day in room service," says Hilton vice president of food and beverage Paul Houdayer. "We try to do the best we can to minimize the waiting period. At times we have as many as fifty room servers, but the room service pressure only lasts two to three hours. Everyone wants to have breakfast from seven to eight in the morning."

The one thing a superhotel can't do as well as a small place is get the food up to the room quickly. "People are going to have to wait thirty minutes; there's no way around that," says Houdayer. "When we have an operation of this size, with the distances we have to travel from one end of the building to the other, it's going to take some time."

The Las Vegas Hilton is right next door to the Convention Center. During big conventions, most businessmen prefer to have meetings in their rooms and order room service for breakfast. At most Strip hotels, however, room service orders are usually for newlyweds. "The first thing they order is a bottle of champagne," says Riviera room service waiter Willie Rodriguez. "Then they order a steak dinner." The most common room service order overall? "Shrimp," says Rodriguez, "fried shrimp or shrimp on ice."

André Beaudry, room-service waiter at the Las Vegas Hilton

Elizabeth Casey, owner of Off-Air
Recording Service

PARKING

In Las Vegas, every hotel/casino does something pretty unusual for a big city: They provide acres and acres of free parking. The only hitch is that you've got to do some serious work to find a space.

The traffic jams at the Circus Circus parking garage can be as bad as any urban drag on a Saturday night. Some hotels provide parking spaces so far away that it seems you've walked a mile once you're arrived panting at the front door. So, many guests partake of one of the world's last great bargains. They pull up to the front door of the hotel and have a parking valet do the job for them. All that's expected in return is a toke—usually $1.

"To be a good valet, you've got to be in shape," says George Vera of Caesars Palace. "You've got to like working outdoors and be able to run fast. The faster you run, the better your tips are going to be."

Vera says Caesars parks a thousand cars on a busy day, with each valet responsible for 150 to 200.

CIVILIAN

Elizabeth Casey is one of a rare breed. She lives in Las Vegas, but has absolutely nothing to do with the casino industry. She doesn't gamble, doesn't drink, doesn't smoke, and stays as far away from the Strip as she can.

And she wouldn't live anywhere else.

Las Vegas has a reputation around the rest of the world we are trying hard to overcome. Everyone *isn't* involved in the casinos. We have the same types of industries as any other town. We have our fair share of lawyers and doctors, gas stations and grocery stores. The only thing we don't have is major, major industries. GM is not here, but then GM is not everywhere. There is a lot here that doesn't have to do with gaming.

Casey moved from New York to Vegas with her two young daughters in the early 1970s after a divorce, when her parents decided to retire there. When she told her friends she was moving to Glitter Gulch, they said, "Las Vegas . . . I didn't know people actually lived there."

"Everybody who lives here has had that conversation," she says. "Not all of us are dancing on the stage every night."

She got a job in the publicity department of the Stardust Hotel, then moved to KNTV's promotion department. She sold real estate for a couple of years, and in 1977 started an off-air TV recording service, the video equivalent of a newspaper clipping service.

Casey has thrived in Las Vegas because the small-town atmosphere of the community made it easy for her to start a business there.

If you put yourself out there and get involved in community activities, then you have a greater opportunity to meet the movers and shakers—much easier than in Los Angeles.

I like Las Vegas now. The twenty-four-hour atmosphere is something you get accustomed to, even if you don't take advantage of it. It's nice to know that you can go out at ten at night and get a loaf of bread if you need to. But Vegas does take a while to get adjusted to, because of the male mentality, because of the casinos, because of the showgirls, because of the cocktail waitresses. They look at me differently. It's very common when you're sitting with a male client in a restaurant for him to say "Hey, sweetie" to the cocktail waitress. You don't find that too often in

Parking valets at Caesars

other cities. That tends to make it more difficult for a woman, especially an unescorted woman, to walk around anywhere, because immediately there is suspicion as to whether she is there on business or pleasure.

Casey never spends time in the casinos. "They're loud and glitzy, and I don't drink or gamble, so I don't see any reason to visit them. But I understand people's attraction to them."

RELIGION IN VEGAS

It's Saturday afternoon at the Guardian Angel Church on the Strip, a half-block from the Desert Inn, Stardust, and Peppermill casinos. It's S.R.O. time. The house seats a thousand, but this afternoon, as usual, there are some five hundred more standing in the aisles and on the steps, listening to Father Edward Anderson's sermon.

"Look at this crowd," says one churchgoer. "It's all gamblers praying for luck."

"You're wrong," says another. "They're in here looking for forgiveness."

There are more churches per capita in Vegas than in any other city. Religion—and gambling—are both big business here. While Los Angeles—some 280 miles away—has a major influence on Vegas, Utah—where no liquor is served in restaurants—is just 60 miles in the other direction. Vegas is the city Brigham Young tried to develop into a Mormon community in the 1800s—the desert was just too hot for crops, so he and his followers went back to Utah. But some 10 percent of the Vegas populace are Mormons, folks who are not allowed to drink, smoke, or gamble, and who are discouraged from working in the gambling pits at the casinos. (They are, however, allowed to invest and manage. E. Parry Thomas, the legendary banker form Valley Bank who has financed at least part of virtually every casino in town, is Mormon, as were the executives who ran Howard Hughes's Summa Corporation, which operated the Frontier, Sands, Desert Inn, Landmark, and Silver Slipper for many years.)

The Guardian Angel Church does more business than any other house of worship in town. It's the Caesars Palace of churches. It also caters primarily to tourists, who pack the halls each

The Guardian Angel Church on the Strip, where visitors pray their luck will change

212

weekend to hear Father Anderson talk about Jesus, after they have spent their evenings gambling and partying.

The bywords of the church: goodness, patience, chastity, peace, charity, and joy. Translated into gambler's terms: Winning at twenty-one is good if you wait it out for the right cards, don't get distracted by a chick, give a toke to the dealer, and walk away happy.

The church on the nastiest street in Sin City.

"We have 100,000 people coming from the outside into Vegas every weekend," says Father Anderson.

It wouldn't be a sin city if those 100,000 weren't looking for sin. Let's face it, in the history of the human race, wherever large numbers gather, there is always someone out there to cater to their vices. It's just a reality. Where tourists gather in large numbers, there are certain things that will follow.

Attendance at the busy mass services on weekends at the Guardian Angel is usually about 70 percent tourists, who drop more casino chips than green dollars into the collection cups. Each week someone from the church hauls the chips to Caesars Palace, which converts them into cash.

At the Guardian Angel, dice and slot players regularly ask Father Anderson to bless their hands. In the church gift shop, people buy candles in the hope that lighting them will bless their bets.

"Percentage-wise," says the Father, "I can assure you, without any hesitation, that there are more candles sold here than at any other church in the world."

The Mormons, who have more churches in town than any other denomination—some twenty-eight—request that members not work in the gaming pits. They prefer hotel and food management jobs. But while they will *tolerate* a pit job, they won't tolerate gambling.

"We have a fundamental belief that people should work hard and earn money," says Brother Tom Tyler of the Church of Jesus Christ of Latter-Day Saints of Vegas. "Gambling is an activity where people try to get something for nothing. More people lose than win. Drinking leads to alcoholism; gambling leads to addiction."

Father Anderson, however, has no problem with those who like to lay down bets—he does it often himself.

The Catholic Church says that a person should work hard, earn money, and take care of the needs of their family. If they have surplus money, the presumption is that a certain portion will go to charity. After that, they may decide to go boating, skiing, or surfing, or may just like to play the machines. They work for that money. If that's what they want to do, that's their decision.

Father Anderson's game? "Sports. You can't win at blackjack or roulette."

The odds are against you. With a football bet, I'm matching my intelligence against someone else's intelligence. I read a lot of what other people read and observe the games on TV and see how they play, and decide what to do next week about the team. [Betting] makes the game more interesting.

In 1986, when the Denver Broncos were up against the New York Giants in the Super Bowl, some Denver fans came to the church and asked one of the women there to let the candles burn all night for the Broncos. She said yes. "After I said Mass, they came up to me outside and told me what the woman had said, and wanted my assurance that I would let the candles burn all night," says Father Anderson. "I told them no. I said, 'What can I do? I'm for the Broncos, but I bet on the Giants. I can't leave those candles lit.' The point is that the Giants won and the Broncos lost. I never bet on who I'm for; I bet on who I think will win."

INDEX

Page numbers in italics refer to illustrations.

Photo Credits